NET-ZERO CARBON

Other Books by the Author

The Looming Energy Crisis

Energy the Sources of Prosperity

Crisis in the MidEast (a novel)

Nothing to Fear

CLEXIT

Carbon Folly

Entrepreneur as CEO

NET-ZERO CARBON

The Climate Policy
Destroying America

Donn Dears

Dears, Donn D.
Net-Zero Carbon, The Climate Policy Destroying America
Includes Index

Energy
Net-zero Carbon
Natural Gas
Wind
Solar
Fossil Fuels
Climate Change

ISBN 978-0-9815119-5-5

Published by Donn Dears LLC
Cover Design by Greg Sharp

Manufactured in the United States

Dedicated to all my grandchildren

Acknowledgments

As always, I must thank those who have helped me by reviewing the manuscript and providing me with important insights and suggestions.

Elliott Seiden noted that the book needed continuity so the reader could move smoothly from one section to the next without losing track of the underlying message.

His experience as Section Chief in the Antitrust Division of the Department of Justice and then as a lawyer in the airline industry allowed him to recognize that the manuscript, as initially written, left the reader puzzled as the text moved from one thought to the next. As a result, I organized the book into three parts, where the parts logically followed each other. Elliott had also contributed to my previous book, *The Looming Energy Crisis*, *Are Blackouts Inevitable*.

I appreciate Dr. Happer reviewing Chapter 10 to ensure I had gotten the science right.

Another group read the manuscript and pointed to areas where it was unclear and needed additional information for the text to be easily understood.

This group, Bill Walton, Bob Harding, and Larry Koenig, provided me with honest comments that helped to make the many technical issues easier to understand.

I also want to thank Greg Sharp for creating a cover that not only was eye-catching but also helped unveil the message contained in Net-zero carbon.

Contents

Illustrations

Figures

Tables

Abbreviations

BEV	Battery Electric Vehicle
BOF	Basic Oxygen Furnace
BRI	Belt and Road Initiative
CAISO	California System Operator
CBAM	Carbon Border Adjustment Mechanism
CCS	Carbon Capture and Sequestration
CCNG	Combined Cycle Natural Gas Power Plant(see NGCC)
CLEW	Clean Energy Wire
CLOUD	Cosmics Leaving Outdoor Droplets
CO2	Carbon Dioxide
COP	Conference of the Parties
CH4	Methane
DRI	Direct Reduction of Iron
EAF	Electric Arc Furnace
EIA	Energy Information Administration
EPA	Environmental Protection Agency
ERCOT	Electric Reliability Council of Texas
ETS	Emissions Trading Scheme
EU	European Union
FERC	Federal Energy Regulatory Commission
FI	Financial Intermediary
GATT	General Agreement on Tariffs and Trade
GHG	Greenhouse Gas
GS	Geologic Sequestration
IEA	International Energy Agency
HELE	High Efficiency Low Emissions
ICE	Internal Combustion Engine

IFC	International Finance Corporation
IPCC	Intergovernmental Panel on Climate Change
ISO	Independent System Operator
ISO-NE	Independent System Operator of New England
LCOE	Levelized Cost of Electricity
LCOE	(alternative) Levelized Cost of Energy
LNG	Liquefied Natural Gas
MIGA	Multilateral Investment Guarantee Agency
NDC	Nationally Determined Contributions
NGCC	Natural Gas Combined Cycle
NGO	Non-Governmental Organizations
NREL	National Renewable Energy Laboratory
PEM	Polymer Electrolyte Membrane
PPA	Public Purchase Agreement
PV	Photo Voltaic
RTO	Regional Transmission Organization
SMR	Steam Methane Reforming
SPM	Summary for Policymakers
UNFCCC	United Nations Framework on Climate Change
WTO	World Trade Organization
WUWT	Watts Up With That

Preface

The United States stands on a precipice, peering down at an abyss of self-destruction.

Net-zero carbon is the policy driving Americans to that abyss.

The United States is currently the preeminent country in the world, with unequaled resources and a capitalist system that creates prosperity, where freedom is protected by the Constitution. No document, similar to the US Constitution exists anywhere else in the world that enshrines, in law, the guarantee of freedom.

Net-zero carbon is based on the false narrative that greenhouse gasses, specifically CO_2, are an existential threat to mankind.

This has created a political movement demanding the elimination of fossil fuels.

But, fossil fuels are the overwhelming source of energy on which economies worldwide are founded.

Politicians have settled on wind and solar and battery-powered vehicles as the means for replacing fossil fuels.

The United Nations Framework Convention on Climate Change (UNFCCC) is the political instrument for organizing this effort worldwide. The Intergovernmental Panel on Climate Change (IPCC), with its investigations into how humans are affecting the climate, creates the fear needed to induce people to accept the pronouncements of the UNFCCC.

The UNFCCC and their supporters have embarked on an effort to transform the world, where wind and solar replace fossil fuels and where virtually everything is powered by electricity, using so-called clean energy.

But, net-zero carbon policies will lead to a world where energy will be in short supply, poverty and death will be more prevalent, and freedom is eradicated.

It requires Americans to trade energy independence, based on oil and natural gas, for dependency on other countries, primarily China, for the minerals needed to support a net-zero carbon economy.

Along the way, freedom will be lost as the government imposes restrictions and mandates to force the elimination of fossil fuels.

This book establishes why net-zero carbon is a trap that will destroy the United States.

It is organized into three Parts. Part 1 defines net-zero carbon and examines how power generation, transportation, and industry, would be affected by attempts to achieve net-zero carbon, including the prospect of using hydrogen.

Part 2 examines the politics behind the effort to eliminate fossil fuels.

Part 3 deals with the realities of climate science and the appalling effects that net-zero carbon policies would have on the United States.

Introduction

There cannot be two suns in the same sky,
nor two emperors on the earth.

Confucius

Net-zero Carbon Issues

The earlier book, *Carbon Folly*, described the difficulties of eliminating CO2 emissions when the book was written. Conditions haven't changed substantially, and the fundamental problems remain unchanged.

Total US CO2 emissions in 2004, as shown in Table 1, from *Carbon Folly*, were somewhat lower than US emissions in 2019.

Table 1		
US CO2 Emissions 2004		
Source	**MMT**	**% Total**
Electric Generation	2298.6	39%
Gasoline	1162.6	20%
Industrial	1069.3	18%
Transportation (excluding gasoline)	771.1	13%
Residential	374.7	6%
Commercial	228.8	4%
Total Untied States	5905.1	100%

Total excludes approximately 70 MMT CO2 emissions from miscellaneous sources.

Source: Emissions of Greenhouse Gases in the United States 2005 by DOE Energy Information Administration.

MMT = Million Metric Tons 1 MMT = 2205 pounds

Table 2 compares Environmental Protection Agency (EPA) 2019 data with Energy Information Administration (EIA) 2004 data.

Table 2 US CO2 Emissions Comparison		
	EPA 2019	**EIA 2004**
Total CO2 MMT	6,558[1]	5,904[2]
Electric Generation %	31	39
Transportation %	35	33
Industrial %	16	18

Emissions from generating electricity have fallen from 39% to 31% of the total, primarily due to a reduction in the number of coal-fired power plants. Meanwhile, transportation emissions have increased.

1. Comparisons aren't exact because the 2004 EIA data didn't include agriculture.

2. The basic issues remain mostly unchanged. CO2 emissions from transportation and the generation of electricity remain the largest contributors.

3. Industrial emissions have increased in importance because they encompass some of the more difficult challenges for eliminating CO2 emissions.

Comparing US emissions with other countries can provide valuable insights into the difficulties of achieving reductions.

It can also show how the actions of other countries affect worldwide CO2 emissions.

Germany

Germany has spent billions of dollars trying to cut CO2 emissions.

Germany has reduced its greenhouse gas (GHG) emissions, i.e., in CO2 equivalents, from 1,020 MMT in 2004, to 810 MMT in 2019.

This is a 20.5% reduction over 15 years.[3]

During the same period, the United States reduced its CO2 emissions 14%, while becoming energy independent using fossil fuels.[4]

China

China has seen its CO2 emissions rapidly increase, with no commitment to cap them until 2030.[5]

China's CO2 emissions have increased from 4,500 MMT in 2004,[6] when they were less than US emissions, to 11,535 MMT in 2019,[7] when they were nearly twice US emissions.

India

India, representative of developing countries, increased its CO2 emissions from 1,087 MMT in 2004, to 2,435 MMT in 2018, a 124% increase.[8]

The premise in *Carbon Folly* was that emissions would have to be reduced 80% by 2050.

The new policy objective is to achieve net-zero carbon emissions by 2050.

Wind and solar are the technologies being promoted to replace fossil fuels, coupled with a strategy of converting everything using fossil fuels to using electricity instead.

Requiring battery-powered vehicles (BEVs) to replace internal combustion engine (ICE) vehicles is one example.

Some people prefer BEVs, which have perceived benefits, such as being quiet.

In a free market, BEVs would increase their share of the market based on consumer acceptance, and if consumers preferred BEVs to ICE vehicles, BEVs would eventually dominate the market.

An orderly transition, such as this, would allow for the development of supply lines that wouldn't leave the United States dependent on China for minerals.

The term carbon is, of course, inaccurate. Carbon refers to a solid substance, such as is used in pencils. Some have said the term was adopted to incite people by having them envision soot rather than having them see that CO_2 is a clear, odorless gas.

The correct terminology is net-zero CO_2 emissions. However, the term carbon will continue to be used herein since it is the term used most frequently by the media.

IPCC AR6

The IPCC released its latest report, *IPCC Sixth Assessment Report* (AR6) and the summary for policymakers (SPM), *Climate Change 2021, Summary for Policy Makers*, in August 2021.

As expected, the summary regurgitated all the terrible things that will happen if the world doesn't achieve net-zero carbon by 2050. It bases these predictions of catastrophes on computer models, but it's been repeatedly shown that computer models have not reliably predicted future temperatures. This will be discussed in Chapter 10.

Nevertheless, AR6 has been used to excite and arouse the participants from 197 countries at the COP 26 meeting in Glasgow, Scotland, during November 2021.

The UNFCCC, and its COP meetings, will be discussed in greater detail in Chapter 7.

The Wall Street Journal's comments on AR6 are appropriate.[9]

> The gargantuan report will take time to plow through, but a read of the 41-page 'summary for policymakers' and perusal of the rest suggests that there is no good reason to sacrifice your life, or even your standard of living, to the climate gods.

and:

> Keep in mind that the IPCC report is a political document. It is intended to scare the public and motivate politicians to reduce CO2 emissions no matter the cost, which by the way the report summary never mentions.

The media will also use the dire warnings from AR6 to instill fear in people, which fosters their acceptance of net-zero carbon policies.

Interestingly, one of the future catastrophes cited in AR6 is sea level rise. This is an area of great interest due to my training and experiences in the Navy and Merchant Marine.

AR6 claims that sea levels will now rise at the rate of 0.1 inches per year.

This is 10 inches in 100 years.

Over the past few hundred years, the actual sea level rise has been approximately 8 inches every 100 years. So while the AR6 projection may amount to a 25% increase, it will hardly be noticed.

The actual cause of apparent sea level rise is subsidence, where the land is sinking, either due to the extraction of water from the water table, or due to isostatic rebound from the last glaciation.

Net-zero carbon, however, would be a true catastrophe for the United States and the American people.

Which brings up the issue of China.

China

China now emits nearly twice as much CO_2 as the United States, i.e., 11,535 vs. 6,558 MMT.

China has pledged to have its CO_2 emissions peak by 2030 and then achieve carbon neutrality by 2060. Carbon neutrality implies net-zero carbon by 2060, but that's not at all clear.

There is no corroborating evidence to confirm China will meet its commitments.

Coal is at the center of any discussion about China's energy use and intentions.

What have been China's recent actions?

In 2019, 58% of China's total energy consumption came from coal, and, in absolute terms, coal's usage increased in 2019.[10]

China added 38.4 GW new coal-fired capacity in 2020, and while some older plants were retired, overall capacity increased by 29.8 GW.[11]

In addition, China initiated 73.5 GW of new coal-fired power plant construction, five times more than the 13.9 GW installed by the rest of the world.[12]

In 2020, assuming an average size of 800 MW per coal-fired power plant, China built 48 new coal-fired power plants and initiated the construction of an additional 92 plants.

These power plants have a life expectancy of 60 years, well past 2060, when China says it will achieve carbon neutrality.

Are these the actions of a country intent on reducing CO2 emissions?

There is an attempt to compare per capita emissions of China and the United States, i.e., 8 vs. 16.1 tons per person, to make it appear as though the United States is the greater culprit.

The atmosphere doesn't care where the CO2 originated or what someone's carbon footprint may be. If CO2 actually affects climate, it's the total emissions that count.

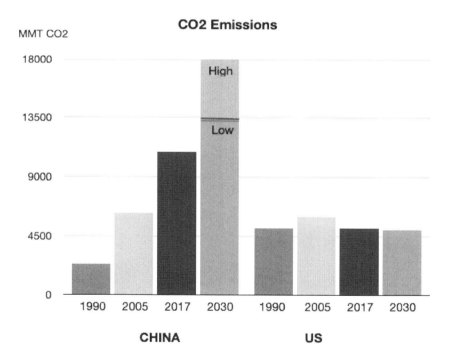

Figure 1, China vs. US CO2 Emissions
China's high estimate is based on Obama-China climate agreement, WUWT, E. Hoskins. Low estimate is from the Center for Climate and Energy Solutions.

Figure 1 shows actual CO2 emissions for China and the United States (1990-2017) and projections for 2030.[13]

It would appear that, by 2030, China will emit three to four times the CO2 emissions of the United States.

In the construct of recent Chinese history, in combination with ancient Chinese philosophies, there is the question of whether China's government is trying to deceive and mislead other countries.

The Hundred-Year Marathon warns that China's ambition is to replace the United States as the global superpower.[14]

As described in *The Hundred-Year Marathon*, China's purpose is to achieve this objective by 2049, the hundred-year anniversary of the communist ascendency to power in China, with the retreat of the Kuomintang to Formosa, i.e., Taiwan.

Historically, Chinese strategy has utilized deception, as illustrated by this quotation, from the *Thirty-Six Stratagems*:[15]

"Deceive the heavens to cross the ocean."

Another quotation, this by Confucius, from *The Hundred-Year Marathon*, is more explicit.

"There cannot be two suns in the same sky,
nor two emperors on the earth."

It would be suicidal for the United States to rely on promises made by Chinese leaders.

China's actions are more important than its words, and thus far, China's actions have undermined confidence in its commitments.

China has gone back on its commitment, enshrined in a treaty, to maintain Hong Kong as an independent entity, and is in the process of eliminating free speech while imprisoning individuals who protest against China's takeover of Hong Kong.

Confirming China's breaching of the treaty, the UK's Foreign Secretary, Dominic Raab, said:

> The Chinese authorities' continued action means I must now report that the UK considers Beijing to be in a state of ongoing non-compliance with the Joint Declaration — a demonstration of the growing gulf between Beijing's promises and its actions.[16]

With respect to climate, China's energy policies have resulted in increased CO_2 emissions, to the point that they are twice as great as those of the United States.

China has staked out strategic positions, such as the Belt and Road Initiative (BRI).

The BRI calls for constructing a land route from China to Europe, and a sea route with installations in countries along the Indian Ocean, to extend China's influence to Southeast Asia and the Asian countries west of China.

Critically important for the future of the United States, China is strategically positioned to be the world's major supplier of minerals needed by the United States to achieve a net-zero carbon economy.

With these thoughts in mind, should the United States adopt a net-zero carbon policy?

Part 1
Eliminating CO2 Emissions

The only thing we have to fear is . . . fear itself.

President Franklin D. Roosevelt

Chapter 1

Net-zero Carbon

The White House established that the policy of the US government is to achieve net-zero carbon emissions by 2050.[17]

The ultimate question needing an answer is whether net-zero carbon, i.e., net-zero CO2, is good for the United States and Americans?

But, what is net-zero carbon? And why isn't it zero carbon?

The administration's goal is the same as the goal promoted by the United Nations.

According to the United Nations, "131 countries have set, or are considering a target of reducing emissions to net-zero, by mid-century."[18]

One problem with a net-zero goal is that it is amorphous.

In many ways, it is a distraction that allows everyone setting such a goal to claim, no matter what their actions, that they have met the goal.

The term "net-zero" infers preventing CO2 from entering the atmosphere or for its removal from the atmosphere.

The theoretical processes to remove CO2 from the atmosphere, or prevent it from reaching the atmosphere, can be grouped as follows.

- Capturing CO2 from where it is produced (carbon capture).
- Using CO2 in a process, such as in the making of steel.
- Sequestering CO2 underground.

- Sequestering CO2 in plants.
- Geoengineering, such as fertilizing the oceans to increase plankton growth to absorb CO2 from the atmosphere.

These concepts are either unproven or have serious limitations or drawbacks.

The net-zero concept is a distraction because the breadth of the proposal is unlimited and leads to conjecture rather than facts.

A few examples are cited here to provide some context to the issue.

Capturing CO2 from NGCC or coal-fired power plants will result in a derating of the plant by around 30%, requiring the building of additional generating capacity to replace the power lost in capturing, compressing, and transporting the liquid CO2 to where it can be sequestered underground.

There can be no assurance that CO2 sequestered underground will remain there for thousands of years. The EPA has approved only two Class VI wells for sequestering CO2 underground in the United States, primarily because of the risks involved with sequestering CO2.

Class VI wells, as defined by the EPA:

> Class VI wells are used to inject carbon dioxide (CO2) into deep rock formations. This long-term underground storage is called geologic sequestration (GS). Geologic sequestration refers to technologies to reduce CO2 emissions to the atmosphere and mitigate climate change.[19]

Quoting the Competitive Enterprise Institute,[20]

> The EPA bases the regulation of CO2 injection as a separate class of wells on several unique risk factors:
>
> - The large volumes of CO2 expected to be injected through wells.
>
> - The relative buoyancy of CO2 in underground geologic formations.

- The mobility of CO2 within subsurface formations.
- The corrosive properties of CO2 in the presence of water that can effect well materials.
- The potential presence of impurities in the injected CO2 stream.

There are examples of where natural gas has leaked from supposedly secure underground geologic storage. There were leaks from underground storage at Aliso Canyon in California,[21] and at Hutchinson, Kansas.[22]

As for sequestering CO2 in plants, such as trees, what happens when the trees or plants are cut down? Or die? Can sequestration, such as planting trees in Mongolia or the Amazon, be honestly certified? For how long? And by whom?

The issues surrounding negative carbon strategies, e.g., CCS and geoengineering, are never-ending, which is why it is a distraction rather than a serious component of any proposal.

Every claim made by any company, organization, or country has to be carefully examined to see what is meant by net-zero.

From a scientific perspective, the term is bogus.

There are other greenhouse gases besides CO2, and they get less attention when discussing net-zero carbon.

It appears as though GHGs, other than CO2, are accounted for by using CO2 equivalents for each specific GHG, e.g., CH4, i.e., methane, and then including them in any determination of net-zero carbon.

The preponderance of media reporting is on CO2 rather than GHG and CO2 equivalents.

The purpose behind net-zero carbon was established by the 2016 Paris Agreement and the IPCC's special report, *Global Warming of 1.5° C,* to prevent the world's temperature from rising by more than 1.5° C above preindustrial levels.[23]

Chapter 10 will explain there is overwhelming evidence there is no need to cut CO2 emissions by any amount and that CO2 emissions are, in fact, beneficial.

Science supports the conclusion that CO2 is not an existential threat to mankind.

Chapter 2

Net-zero for Power Generation

The basic argument for achieving net-zero carbon is simple: Stop using fossil fuels for generating electricity.

The reality is more complex.

There is the question of whether it is technically possible to eliminate fossil fuels. This book will proceed by assuming it is possible, though there is overwhelming evidence it is not.

A compelling reason supporting the contention that it is not technically possible to abandon fossil fuels is that there is no battery in existence that can store large quantities of electricity for long enough periods of time to ensure grid reliability.

When asked about batteries in an interview, former Secretary of Energy Moniz, an Obama appointee, said,

"Batteries will never be the solution for long-term storage."[24]

Obviously, new technologies may be developed that will allow the storage of electricity for long periods.

Recently, a start-up company, Form Energy Inc., announced it had developed a revolutionary new battery for use on the grid that could provide longe-term storage. It uses inexpensive iron-ore pellets to store electricity. The company says the battery can provide power for 150 hours, or 6.2 days, which would be revolutionary.[25]

Even so, 6.2 days is less than half the length of time needed to prevent blackouts. Moreover, as will be explained later, there have been instances where wind and solar have been virtually unavailable for longer than 14 days.

Even 14 days may not be enough.

Achieving net-zero carbon for generating electricity relies on wind and solar, in combination with batteries for storage, where wind and solar will replace virtually all fossil fuels.

There is also the question of hydrogen.

Many utilities, who have made net-zero commitments, assume they will be able to continue using gas turbine power plants to back up wind and solar while providing electricity as in the past, by using hydrogen.

Gas turbines that use natural gas can be retrofitted to use hydrogen.

Hydrogen burns ten times more rapidly than natural gas, and as a result, the hydrogen flame can extend back to the fuel nozzle, causing damage to the equipment. The combustor, or combustion chamber, can be modified during the retrofitting to accommodate hydrogen.

Chapter 5 provides critical information about hydrogen; information everyone needs to know before assuming hydrogen is the solution to achieving net-zero carbon goals.

Nuclear is left to die on the vine because too many environmentalists oppose nuclear power. As it stands today, all existing nuclear power plants will have been shut down by 2060, and only the two now under construction in Georgia will remain in operation if they are completed.[26]

Wind and solar are unreliable and more costly than fossil fuels, yet they are being relied on to create a net-zero carbon grid.

Reliability, cost, and the need to double generating capacity by 2050 to meet the net-zero carbon objective will be examined next.

Reliability

Grid reliability is crucial for the safety of all Americans. The recent Texas blackouts made this clear to everyone. People in Texas died because they couldn't get electricity.

The formation of Regional Transmission Organizations (RTOs) and Independent System Operators (ISOs), under the direction of the Federal Energy Regulatory Commission (FERC) in 1999, created an environment in which reliability became an issue.

Originally intended to create competition to lower cost, RTO/ISOs have evolved in such a way that they have increased cost and reduced grid reliability.

The ideologically driven desire of RTO/ISOs to increase wind and solar on the grid, so as to replace fossil fuels, has resulted in higher costs and less grid reliability.[27]

Figure 2 identifies the RTO/ISOs responsible for managing the grid for two-thirds of the country. Traditionally regulated utilities manage the remaining third of the country.

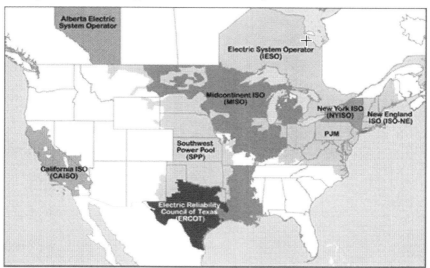

Figure 2, RTO/ISOs

Traditionally regulated utilities determine how much generating capacity is needed to guarantee reliability and then propose this to the regulators in that state. The regulators approve or modify the proposal and then approve a rate, i.e., price, for electricity that would provide a fair rate of return on the required investment.

The RTO/ISOs do not generate electricity. Instead, their primary function is to determine which suppliers of electricity are to be used during each day; and establish procedures for ensuring utilities build enough new generating capacity to maintain reliable operation of the grid. RTO/ISOs also provide ancillary services, such as keeping the flow of electricity at a frequency of 60 cycles per second, within extremely tight limits.

The book, *The Looming Energy Crisis, Are Blackouts Inevitable,* explains in detail how RTO/ISOs function.

RTO/ISO activities:

- RTO/ISOs conduct day-ahead auctions where suppliers bid to have their electricity used on the grid. They then conduct real-time auctions the next day to fill in any unexpected gaps in supply.

- Most RTO/ISOs hold capacity auctions to ensure there is enough generating capacity available in the next few years to meet demand.

- RTO/ISOs also manage ancillary services, such as frequency control, to ensure the smooth operation of the grid within their geographic area.

- RTO/ISOs are, essentially, bureaucracies established to manage the operation of the grid within specific geographic areas.

- Electric utilities in these areas are relegated to being suppliers without being responsible for reliability.

The grid must be kept in balance, where the supply of electricity always meets demand, second by second. Any slight deviation from this prerequisite and the grid will fail.

Wind and solar are intermittent and cannot be relied on to supply electricity on-demand. Reserve capacity is required to prevent blackouts and must be available on-demand. It must be available when needed.

Every utility should have adequate reserve margins to ensure electricity is available if demand increases beyond prior peaks in demand, or if power generation equipment fails.

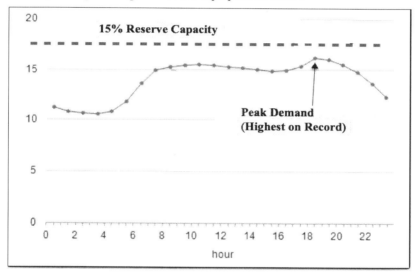

Figure 3, Diagram showing reserve capacity
with 15% reserve margin.

Only baseload power plants should be used for reserve capacity, and only coal-fired, natural gas combined cycle, or nuclear plants are baseload plants because they are available 24/7, 365 days a year.

The Texas blackouts were, at least in part, due to reliance on wind for reserve capacity.

ERCOT (Electric Reliability Council of Texas) issued a report in December, immediately preceding the blackouts, that the Texas grid had a 15.5% reserve margin. Actually, there was no reserve capacity using baseload power.[28] An earlier report had predicted a near-zero reserve margin in 2021 with baseload power.[29]

California has also experienced blackouts.

The California Independent System Operator (CAISO) has been relying on solar and wind to supply California with electricity, with the objective of achieving 100% net-zero CO_2 emissions by 2050.

CAISO has been calling for the closure of natural gas power plants while also forcing the premature closure of nuclear power plants.

For example, the San Onofre nuclear power plant was closed in 2013, and Diablo units 1 and 2, the last two nuclear power plants in California, are scheduled for closure in 2024 and 2025.

To cover these shortfalls in baseload power, CAISO has been relying on electricity imported from surrounding states, and obtained FERC's approval to divert hydropower from the Pacific Northwest that had been contracted for by Arizona.[30]

In essence, CAISO has been expecting surrounding states to invest in baseload power so that California could institute policies that cut CO_2 emissions.

California will continue to experience blackouts as long as they lack sufficient baseload reserve capacity.

Other RTO/ISOs have established rigged auctions to force wind and solar onto their systems, which has also resulted in the closing of nuclear power plants.[31]

Capacity auctions are supposed to ensure reliable future capacity. But RTO/ISOs are attempting to allow wind and solar to be included in capacity auctions which would threaten grid reliability.

Wind and solar cannot be relied on to provide guaranteed capacity, even with battery storage.

Efforts to achieve net-zero carbon by replacing fossil fuels with wind and solar will result in a less reliable grid and more blackouts, which will endanger the lives of all Americans.

The Independent System Operator of New England (ISO-NE) narrowly averted a blackout in the winter of 2018 by using oil as a backup fuel for natural gas power plants and came within hours of having the oil run out, which would have meant blackouts.

Wind and solar provided pathetically small amounts of electricity during this sixteen-day period. Figure 4 shows the actual solar output during this emergency.

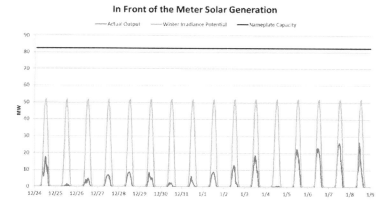

Figure 4, In Front of Meter Solar Generation
From ISO-New England Cold Weather Operations Presentation,
January 2018[32]
Top curve anticipated output. Bottom curve actual output.

From December 25, when there was virtually no electricity generated by solar, until January 4, when, again, there was no electricity generated by solar, the generation of electricity from solar was almost nonexistent for ten of the sixteen days.

Unbelievably, FERC ruled that ISO-NE could not use oil as a backup fuel in the future because of fuel neutrality.[33]

Attempting to achieve net-zero carbon will impair grid reliability and endanger all Americans.

Cost

The cost of wind and solar has been misrepresented by the media and climate activists, including those organizations and institutions adhering to the claim that CO2 is an existential threat to mankind.

It should be obvious that electricity produced by wind and solar costs more than that produced by coal-fired, natural gas combined cycle and existing nuclear power plants.

Wind and solar must have backup, with baseload power plants in spinning reserve mode, i.e., in operation but not connected to the grid, ready to come on line at a moment's notice when the wind stops blowing or the sun stops shining, or by using storage.

As already noted, there is no battery in existence that can store enough electricity for a long enough period to ensure reliable operation of the grid.

Batteries can be used for short-term storage to back up wind and solar, similar to spinning reserves.

Batteries cost money, and their cost should be added to the cost of wind and solar when evaluating total costs.

The majority of costs quoted by the media and activists omit the cost of backup, including storage.

The levelized cost of electricity (LCOE) is the usual metric for comparing costs, and the LCOEs for wind and solar, quoted by the media, almost always exclude the cost of backup. *Almost*, so as not to be cited for misrepresenting the facts, as there may have been an instance where backup costs were included, somewhere.

The cost of storage is excluded from LCOE calculations because storage is paid for separately, usually by the electric utility and not by the company generating the electricity. It's also the established procedure since, historically, storage was not needed to back up coal-fired, natural gas, or nuclear power plants.

Some organizations have gone to great lengths developing LCOEs for wind and solar to establish their low cost. Lazard, for example, is frequently cited as the source of such information.

Lazard's procedures are conspicuously flawed and appear to misrepresent fundamental data.[34] In addition, Lazard's LCOEs also exclude the cost of backup.

LCOEs for existing power plants are typically lower than for new plants. For example, the LCOE for existing natural gas combined cycle (NGCC) power plants is 3.6 cents per kWh, while LCOEs for new NGCC plants is 5 cents per kWh.[35]

This is an important consideration. Closing existing power plants with low LCOEs, whether coal-fired or nuclear, and replacing them with higher-cost new power plants, increases the cost of electricity for everyone.

Public purchase agreements (PPA) have also been cited to establish that wind and solar are less costly, but these lower prices are frequently the result of subsidies. Note also that they do not include the cost of backup.

Wind and solar power plants must also be replaced far more frequently than coal-fired, natural gas, or nuclear power plants.

Wind and PV solar installations are expected to last for 20 to 25 years. Nuclear power plants last for 80 years, while NGCC and coal-fired power plants last for at least 60 years. Batteries also only last for 10 to 15 years.

The short useful lives of wind, PV solar, and batteries, essentially triples the total investment required for wind and PV solar when compared with coal-fired, natural gas, and nuclear power plants.

Doubling Generating Capacity

Finally, it won't be sufficient to merely replace the existing power generation capacity, enormous as that task is. Instead, it will be necessary to double the generating capacity of the United States and increase the size of the transmission and distribution systems as well.

The 2021 *Electrification Futures Study*[36] by the national renewable energy laboratory (NREL), established that requiring all new vehicles to be battery-powered and all heating to be electric will require a doubling of power generation capacity in the United States.

Replacing all existing power plants, plus the new plants required for battery-powered vehicles and electric heating of homes, with wind and PV solar, including the batteries needed for backup, is estimated to cost $7.5 trillion every twenty years.[37]

This cost approximates one-third of the United States debt, repeated every twenty years, which is the life expectancy of wind, solar, and battery installations.

Committing to net-zero carbon is financially unsustainable and will bankrupt the country.

Chapter 3

Net-zero for Transportation

Not only will new power generation, transmission, and distribution capacity be needed if all light vehicles in the United States are battery-powered (BEVs), but an entirely new supply chain needs to be developed.

The initial problem is that the leadership in battery technology lies in Asia, primarily in China, Japan, and South Korea.

The next problem, which is even more tenacious, is that the materials needed to manufacture lithium-ion batteries must be imported.

Finally, there is the problem of building the manufacturing and other infrastructure, such as battery charging stations, needed to support the adoption of BEVs in the United States, with the concomitant discontinuance of internal combustion (ICE) vehicle manufacturing.

There is the additional issue of how to end the use of fossil fuels by heavy-duty trucks, railroads, and airplanes since batteries are ill-suited for these applications.

Fuel cells, hydrogen, and biofuels have been proposed as solutions for these modes of transportation.

The hydrogen needed for fuel cells and the biofuels required for aviation both have huge hurdles to overcome.

There is the need for even more electricity to produce hydrogen, as well as a myriad of other problems, including the transport of hydrogen, which bedevil any attempt for its use.[38]

The primary problem with biofuels is the lack of feedstock to produce enough aviation fuel to support a robust airline industry. Proposed feedstocks include kitchen grease, trees, garbage, and algae. Each is analyzed for the adequacy of supply in Chapter 10, *Nothing to Fear.*[39]

There is not enough feedstock to support the use of biofuels in place of jet fuel.

Hydrogen and biofuels are both very speculative and border on fantasy rather than fact.

BEVs have been proven to work and have features that appeal to enthusiasts and average consumers.

In addition, major manufacturers have said they will discontinue manufacturing ICE vehicles by 2035. For example, General Motors (GM) announced in January 2021, "It aspires to eliminate tailpipe emissions from new light-duty vehicles by 2035."[40]

There is a possibility ICE vehicles will be eliminated, and Americans will be forced to buy BEVs.

How will this affect the United States?

Battery Technology

Each major manufacturer has announced plans to build plants in the United States to manufacture lithium-ion batteries.

General Motors has announced it will invest $35 billion through 2025 in BEVs. Ford has announced it will invest $22 billion through 2025.

Fiat Chrysler has announced it will use A123 systems, a Chinese-controlled company, as its battery supplier.

GM and Ford have aligned themselves with LG Chem and SK Innovation, respectively, to build batteries in the United States.

These are both South Korean companies. Panasonic, another battery manufacturer based in Japan, is aligned with Tesla.

US battery manufacturers are currently importing battery cells from Asia and assembling them in specific battery configurations suitable for their vehicles.

Battery cells must be built in the United States, not Asia; otherwise, the United States will remain dependent on Asia for battery cells and the technology needed to advance their design. Even the GM Lordstown factory will have LG Chem making the battery cells for GM to package.

China, Japan, and South Korea lead in battery technology, with the United States scrambling to catch up.

Battery Materials

Even if the United States catches up with the technology and can build enough lithium-ion batteries to serve the market, the United States will still be dependent on foreign countries for the materials.

The International Energy Agency (IEA) has made it clear that BEVs will use more materials than ICE vehicles.

Quoting from the executive summary of their report, *The Role of Critical Mineral in Clean Energy Transitions*:

> "A typical electric car requires six times the mineral inputs of a conventional car."

The IEA has itemized the countries that provide the extraction and processing of these critical minerals and the percentage of world demand they supply. See Table 3.[41]

Table 3		
Mineral Extraction and Processing Sources		
Metal	**Extraction - Country (%)**	**Processing - Country (%)**
Copper	**Chile (28)**, Peru, (12) China (7)	**China (40)**, Chile (10), Japan (3)
Nickel	**Indonesia (32)**, Philippines (12), Russia (10)	**China (37)**, Indonesia (8), Japan (4)
Cobalt	**DRC (70)**, Russia (3), Australia (2)	**China (63)**, Finland (5), Belgium (4)
Rare Earths	**China (60)**, US (7), Myanmar (6)	**China (83)**, Malaysia (7)
Lithium	**Australia (52)**, Chile (11), China (5)	**China (58)**, Chile (15), Argentina (5)
Note: % = Approximate percentage of world supply, with largest in boldface. DRC = Democratic Republic of the Congo		

The outlook for additional mines in the United States is bleak due to environmental regulations and resistance by environmentalists and others.

A recent example is a lawsuit by Native American tribes to stop Lithium Americas Corp. from excavating its Thacker Pass lithium mine site in Nevada.[42]

Lawsuits against mining in the United States are widespread.

According to the IEA report, each BEV uses approximately 310 pounds of these critical materials.[43]

There are approximately 253 million light vehicles on the road in the United States today.

If all these light vehicles are replaced with BEVs by 2050, a total of 39 million tons of critical materials will be needed by the United States to produce the batteries needed by these BEVs.

Annual usage would be 2.6 million tons, assuming sales of 17 million light vehicles per year.

Battery design could result in material substitutions, such as manganese for nickel, which could result in fewer resources, but for the most part, the materials will still have to be imported.

Solid-state lithium-ion batteries may replace current designs, affecting the mix of materials and their source; however, the United States will still be dependent on foreign countries for materials.

Without new mining facilities in the United States, the US will remain dependent on foreign countries.

Infrastructure

There were approximately 250,000 BEVs sold in 2019. Sales will have to grow at a rate of 25% each year for BEVs to eliminate nearly all ICE vehicles from the road by 2050, assuming light vehicle sales of 17 million vehicles per year.

The reported capacity of GM's Lordstown factory is 30 gigawatt hours.[44] Assuming the average BEV will use a 70 kWh battery, around 40 similar factories will be required in the United States to provide the batteries for the 17 million BEVs sold each year.

At a reported cost of $2.3 billion for the Lordstown factory,[45] the total investment required to build all the battery factories needed in the United States will be around $90 billion.

Based on GM's reported anticipated employment of 1,300 people at its battery factory, the total employment at all 40 battery factories would be around 52,000.

This compares with the approximately 100,000 people employed making ICE engines and transmissions, whose jobs will be displaced by BEVs.

In addition to the cost of building battery factories, there is also the additional cost of building the charging infrastructure to accommodate 253 million BEVs.

Fast charging DC stations, which can charge BEVs in 20 minutes, can cost from $10,000 to $40,000.[46] Fast charging stations will likely be the type sought after by most people, other than when they can charge at home or their place of employment.

No one knows how many charging stations will be required or how many of each type will be needed. However, there are around 125,000 gasoline stations in the United States, so the cost of installing a sufficient number of charging stations of the type needed to satisfy customer time constraints could be billions, possibly a trillion dollars.

Achieving a net-zero carbon strategy to eliminate all ICE vehicles by 2050 subjugates the United States to the whims of foreign material suppliers.

America's supply chain for the automotive industry will be at risk.

In addition, achieving net-zero carbon will impose the added cost on Americans of building battery factories to replace existing engine and transmission factories, as well as the additional cost of creating a charging infrastructure to replace gasoline service stations.

Americans will be replacing factories and gasoline stations that are in good operating condition merely to achieve net-zero carbon.

Chapter 4

Net-zero for Industry

Two industries, in particular, stand in the way of achieving the net-zero carbon goal. They are the steel and cement industries.

Together they account for around 15% of the world's CO_2 emissions. Estimates vary, but steel accounts for approximately 9% and cement for about 6%.[47]

Steel

Currently, there are two predominant methods for producing steel.

- The first uses a basic oxygen furnace (BOF), where pig iron from a blast furnace is converted to molten steel by removing carbon with oxygen. Approximately 80% of the CO_2 emissions are from the blast furnaces, 20% from coking ovens, and a small amount from the BOF.

- The second method uses an electric arc furnace (EAF), where scrap steel is melted using an arc created by an electric arc furnace transformer. This process is nearly free of CO_2 emissions but depends on the availability of scrap steel.

Approximately 75% of the world's steel is made using blast furnaces and the BOF process, while 25% is made using EAFs. A small amount of steel has been made using the direct reduction of iron (DRI) process with natural gas. A tiny amount has been made by replacing coking coal with charcoal.

The steel industry is pursuing two approaches for eliminating these CO_2 emissions.

- The first relies on carbon capture and sequestration (CCS) while continuing to use blast furnaces and BOFs.

- The second uses the Direct Reduction of Iron (DRI) process with hydrogen, rather than natural gas, as the reducing agent.

Relying on CCS is very questionable because there is no guarantee the CO_2 will remain sequestered for centuries. There is also a very high cost for liquifying the CO_2, transporting the liquid CO_2 to where it can be sequestered underground, and then pumping the liquid CO_2 underground. See Appendix.

The DRI alternative using hydrogen is very expensive.

Using either method significantly increases the cost of steel.

Cement

Cement uses limestone and other clay-like materials, which are heated in a kiln at 1400°C, and then ground to form a lumpy, solid substance called clinker. The clinker is combined with gypsum to form cement.

Heating limestone releases CO_2 directly, while burning fossil fuels to heat the kiln also results in CO_2 emissions. Hydrogen could be used instead of fossil fuels, but this increases the cost substantially.

Roughly 50% of the CO_2 emissions from the making of cement are from the limestone, and these emissions must be captured and sequestered underground.

Producing hydrogen is fraught with problems, including the need for additional green electricity.

A more thorough description of the steel and cement making processes, and the problems associated with the production and use of hydrogen, is found in the special report, *Hydrogen and Climate Change*.[48]

Additional Processes and Products

There are other processes in manufacturing that release CO_2. Heat treating of metals, for example, uses natural gas, which would have to be replaced with hydrogen.

The production of plastics require fossil fuels, therefore the extraction and processing of oil and natural gas can't be eliminated if plastics are to be made.

A partial list of other products relying on fossil fuels include:

- Asphalt for highways and roads: (Cement is a substitute but emits CO_2)

- Epoxy: Essential for insulating wiring in electric motors

- Helium: In extractable quantities, is only found in natural gas

- Oil for insulation and cooling of power transformers

- Pharmaceuticals: Produced from fossil fuels

- MRI: Helium for cooling

It's doubtful, modern society can function without fossil fuels.

Chapter 5

Hydrogen

The European Union (EU) has already conceded it can't achieve its net-zero carbon objective without using hydrogen.

It has developed strategies for implementing hydrogen as a necessary component of its net-zero carbon policy.[49]

Recognizing that Europe is too far north to use solar for generating the electricity needed for electrolysis, one plan calls for a vast hydrogen backbone pipeline stretching from North Africa and the Mideast to as far north as Finland.[50]

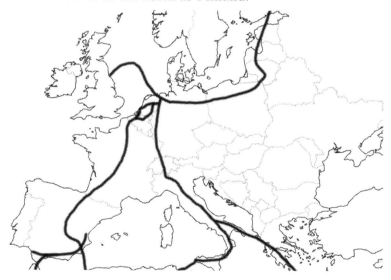

Figure 5, Graphic representation
of proposed European hydrogen pipeline

The following information is taken from *Hydrogen and Climate Change*, a special report published on www.powerforusa.com. The full report contains considerably more detailed information as well as additional diagrams.

The issues surrounding the production and use of hydrogen include:

- Producing hydrogen
- Cost of producing hydrogen
- Quantity of hydrogen needed
- Water requirements
- Storing hydrogen
- Transporting hydrogen

Hydrogen is highly reactive and rarely found in a free state, so it is nearly always found combined with other elements. The most common compound is water, H_2O.

The two primary methods for producing hydrogen are:

- Steam methane reforming (SMR) from natural gas. Nearly all hydrogen is currently made with methane reforming, which results in the release of CO_2.

- Electrolysis, which requires large quantities of electricity, is the method receiving the most attention from climate activists.

Since methane gas is an anathema to those who believe climate change is a catastrophic threat, they insist on using electrolysis with the electricity sourced from renewables.

The various methods for producing hydrogen have given rise to a tier of hydrogens, described as:

- Grey hydrogen, made from methane using steam methane reforming (SMR).
- Brown hydrogen, produced from coal gas.

- Blue hydrogen, made from methane gas using SMR with CO2 capture and sequestration.
- Green hydrogen, produced from water using electrolysis where the electricity is generated by renewables, such as wind and solar.

Hydrogen is a gas at room temperatures and pressures, but can be converted to a supercooled liquid at -453 degrees F. Converting hydrogen to a liquid results in a loss of around 30% of its energy content.

- Current cost of grey hydrogen, using SMR without CCS: $2.08/kg = $0.95/pound.[51]

- Current cost of green hydrogen, using electrolysis: $6.00/kg = $2.73/pound.[52]

The cost of green hydrogen when using electricity produced by wind and solar will vary depending on such things as capacity factor, capital cost, and insolation levels.

In addition, the cost will also vary based on the capital cost of the PEM electrolyzer.

The Department of Energy's target for green hydrogen is $2.00/kg or $0.91/pound.

It is difficult to reconcile DOE's optimistic cost forecast with the very large recurring investment required to produce the green electricity needed to produce the hydrogen when wind turbines and solar installations have to be replaced every twenty years.

It requires between 50 and 55 kWh of electricity to produce 1 kg, or 2.2 pounds, of hydrogen.

Assuming it requires 53 kWh to produce 2.2 pounds of hydrogen, it will require 8,315 billion kWh of electricity to produce the hydrogen needed to replace the natural gas used by the United States annually for all purposes other than industrial uses, such as feedstocks for making plastics.

This amount of electricity is 5.1 times the amount of electricity produced, i.e., 1,617 billion kWh, by existing NGCC power plants in the United States during 2020.[53]

The report determined that 430 billion pounds of hydrogen are needed to replace the natural gas, not used for feedstocks, consumed by the United States. Using electrolysis will require 1,500,000 acre-feet of water to produce 430 billion pounds of hydrogen.[54]

Water requirements are a mismatch with solar-generated electricity in America's Southwest.

Areas conducive to generating electricity from the sun generally lack the necessary supplies of water.

While it's possible to store limited quantities of hydrogen above ground in pressure or cryogenic vessels, large-scale storage will be essential.

Storing hydrogen in salt caverns is being done now, so this storage method can be taken for granted.

However, storing hydrogen safely in other geologic formations is not a certainty. See Appendix on CCS.

The permeability of hydrogen is such that it can leak into spaces natural gas cannot. Hence, while natural gas has been stored in exhausted oil reservoirs and in other geologic formations, it is not proof that hydrogen can be stored in the same formations.

Pipelines transport natural gas around the continental United States to local communities where local gas companies distribute the gas through service lines to residences and businesses.

There are over 305,000 miles of interstate and intrastate pipelines, with 1,400 compressor stations to maintain pressure.[55]

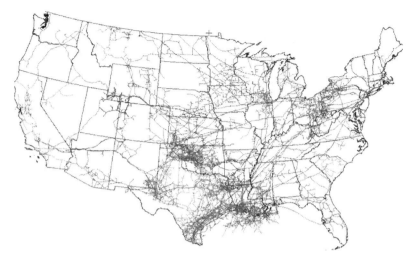

Figure 6, US natural gas pipeline network in 2009 (EIA)

If hydrogen is to be used in place of natural gas, it must be able to reach several hundred natural gas power plants spread across nearly all the states.[56]

It will need to be distributed to over one hundred additional locations spread across the country if it is to be used in steel mills and cement plants and heat-treating facilities in manufacturing plants.

And if it is to be used in airplanes, it will need to be able to reach a thousand airports.

Some publications touting the use of hydrogen say that the existing natural gas pipeline system can be used for transporting hydrogen.

But this is very misleading.

The National Renewable Energy Laboratory (NREL) published a report, *Blending Hydrogen into Natural Gas Pipeline Networks: A Review of Key Issues,* that determined the maximum amount of hydrogen that can be transported by pipeline is a mixture of 20% hydrogen and 80% natural gas.[57]

It is not safe to transport 100% hydrogen in existing pipelines.

Hydrogen is more likely than natural gas to react chemically with other materials. The hydrogen molecule is also smaller than the methane molecule, allowing hydrogen to penetrate materials more readily.

Another safety consideration is whether end-use appliances, e.g., stoves and gas furnaces, can safely use a blend of hydrogen and natural gas. The report said some appliances in Europe would have to be replaced with blends as low as 3% hydrogen. American appliances were not mentioned, but the question remains, what is a safe level for hydrogen when blended with natural gas? The report also said, "For poorly adjusted appliances, no hydrogen blends would be acceptable."

For all intents and purposes, this eliminates the use of gas appliances, with the use of hydrogen restricted to industrial and power generation applications.

Other safety problems include:

- Pipelines made from steel can degrade, e.g., hydrogen embrittlement, when exposed to hydrogen, creating leaks or other failures.
- Plastic pipes, i.e., in distribution or service lines, can allow hydrogen to leak through pipe walls.
- Hydrogen is several times more likely than natural gas to leak through seals.

The report repeatedly emphasizes, "a detailed investigation for every case is mandatory."

If the objective is to eliminate, not just reduce the use of natural gas, the transport of hydrogen using blending of any amount is inappropriate.

Transporting liquified hydrogen by truck, rail, ship, or barge is possible. However, this requires cooling the hydrogen to -453 degrees F. Converting hydrogen to a liquid results in the loss of around 30% of its energy content.

A loss of 30% of its energy makes transporting hydrogen by truck, etc., a bad choice in most situations.

Hydrogen can also be transported as a component of one of the following compounds.[58]

- Ammonia
- Methanol
- Toluene

Transportation of these materials would be by rail, truck, ship, or barge and would not be suitable for distributing hydrogen across the United States to the many geographically dispersed points of use.

Conclusions

Pure, i.e., 100%, hydrogen cannot be safely transported by the nation's existing natural gas pipeline network. Using the natural gas pipeline network to transport pure hydrogen would place American lives at risk.

As a result, it is impossible to safely replace all of the natural gas used by the United States with hydrogen without building an entirely new pipeline network.

While hydrogen could conceivably be used in local or regional settings to eliminate CO2 emissions in the steel industry and reduce CO2 emissions from the making of cement, the cost and complexity of doing so makes little sense.

A local or regional strategy makes no sense for distributing hydrogen to airports since airports are widely dispersed and large in number.

The nation's pipeline network is bound to become an issue as climate activists pursue the elimination of fossil fuels, because it is the only way to distribute hydrogen to the widely dispersed locations where hydrogen is needed.

There is the possibility that new studies will attempt to demonstrate that the natural gas pipeline network is safe for distributing pure hydrogen.

While any study can make assumptions, it cannot change the physical properties of steel or plastic pipes, or the size of the hydrogen molecule.

The fact is, pure hydrogen, or even a mixture of natural gas and hydrogen, should not be transported in the nation's natural gas pipeline network.

Safely storing hydrogen in natural geologic formations, other than salt domes, is also questionable since the permeability of hydrogen is such that it can leak into spaces natural gas cannot.

Water consumption is also an important issue. Using water to produce hydrogen transforms water into oxygen and hydrogen, consuming it in the process. It is entirely different from using water in a power plant where 90% of the water is returned to its source.

Western states, especially in the Southwest, are already stressed for adequate supplies of water. As a result, they are in no position to use solar-generated electricity in electrolyzers to produce hydrogen.

Hydrogen is no panacea for achieving net-zero carbon objectives.

Part 2

The Politics
Behind CO2

We need to stop the mythic fantasies,
and we need to stop the doomsday predictions.
We need to start doing hard science instead.

Michael Crichton

Chapter 6

Reckless Environmentalism

"Today, one of the most powerful religions in the Western World is environmentalism. Environmentalism seems to be the religion of choice for urban atheists. Why do I say it's a religion? Well, just look at the beliefs. If you look carefully, you see that environmentalism is, in fact, a perfect 21st-century remapping of traditional Judeo-Christian beliefs and myths.

There's an initial Eden, a paradise, a state of grace and unity with nature, there's a fall from grace into a state of pollution as a result of eating from the tree of knowledge, and as a result of our actions, there is a judgment day coming for us all. We are all energy sinners, doomed to die, unless we seek salvation, which is now called sustainability. Sustainability is salvation in the church of the environment."

> Remarks to the Commonwealth Club
> by Michael Crichton, San Francisco,
> September 15, 2003.

Michael Crichton was a remarkable person. He received his MD from Harvard Medical school and wrote several famous books, including *Jurassic Park*, *The Andromeda Strain*, and *The Great Train Robbery*. He was a scientist by training and calling.

One more short quote from his talk is relevant.

"I can tell you that the evidence for global warming is far weaker than its proponents would ever admit."

His Commonwealth Club speech was prescient, as we are now ensnared in the climate change debacle.

The trap was set at the Rio Conference, referred to as the Earth Summit, in 1992.

The United Nations Framework Convention on Climate Change (UNFCCC) was adopted at the conference and then ratified by the United States Senate on October 15, 1992.[59]

The treaty's purpose is to cut CO2 emissions, as set forth by Article 2 — Objective:

> The ultimate objective of this Convention and any related legal instruments that the Conference of the Parties may adopt is to achieve, in accordance with the relevant provisions of the Convention, stabilization of greenhouse gas concentrations in the atmosphere at a level that would prevent dangerous anthropogenic interference with the climate system. Such a level should be achieved within a time-frame sufficient to allow ecosystems to adapt naturally to climate change, to ensure that food production is not threatened and to enable economic development to proceed in a sustainable manner.

The objective, i.e., stabilization of greenhouse gasses in the atmosphere, boils down to eliminating fossil fuels, the primary source of greenhouse gasses, including oil, coal, and natural gas. Natural gas, being nearly pure methane.

The UNFCCC treaty calls for annual meetings of member countries, referred to as Conference of the Parties (COP).

These annual meetings have been held in cities around the world, enticing each country to become part of the movement to cut CO2 emissions. Naturally, each country sends representatives who are supportive of the UNFCCC's objective.

There is seldom any real debate over the cause of climate change.

In Bali, the US delegation wanted to object to a proposed agreement and was booed by the attendees.

Each COP meeting has attendees from all 197 member countries. In addition, non-governmental organizations (NGOs) are also allowed to attend, and to some extent, participate in the meetings.

The UNFCCC also established, within COP, two subsidiary bodies to provide technical and management support.

- The Subsidiary Body for Implementation (SBI)
- The Subsidiary Body for Scientific and Technological Advice (SBSTA)

COP acts as judge and jury concerning climate change issues. Resolution of disputes is either by the International Court of Justice or by arbitration through a group appointed from among the 197 member countries.

The United States has one vote among the 197 members.

The International Court should not be able to rule on issues involving United States sovereignty. However, the United States has apparently ceded this authority to the International Court by ratifying the UNFCCC treaty.

Arbitration by members that support cutting CO2 emissions will hardly provide objective rulings.

Each COP meeting is a spectacle involving as many as ten thousand people flying from countries around the world to meeting locations such as Bali, Indonesia; Durban, South Africa; Nairobi, Kenya; and Buenos Aires, Argentina.

If CO_2 was a real threat, COP meetings could be held less frequently, with fewer people, or using web conferences that have been available for at least a dozen years.

It was at COP 21 in 2015 that the Paris Agreement to limit global warming to below 1.5° C was reached.

The Rio conference has been transformed into a powerful movement. A juggernaut that is sweeping away opposition and enveloping countries, organizations, and individuals within its grasp.

There are 197 countries, signatories to the UNFCCC treaty, who have adopted the Paris Agreement. However, of these, only 52, i.e., 26%, have committed to achieving net-zero carbon by 2050. Only 16 of the 52, i.e. 8% of the total, have incorporated their commitment in law, while the remaining 36 merely include their commitment in a non-binding policy document.[60]

Policy documents are easy to write and easy to ignore.

Two countries, Surinam and Bhutan, claim to have achieved net-zero carbon.

- Bhutan claims its forests will sequester all of its CO_2 emissions, while exports of hydropower will contribute to CO_2 reductions.[61]
- Surinam claims its forests will sequester all its CO_2 emissions.[62]

The remaining 144 countries are merely thinking about making a commitment. Officially, as cited by the UNFCCC, their commitment is a "Target Under Discussion."[63]

(This data is for just prior to COP 26 when members increased their commitments for the sake of publicity six years after Paris.)

With three-quarters of all member nations merely thinking about taking action, one must question how critical the climate emergency really is.

The Paris Agreement to cut CO2 emissions was made in December 2015, nearly six years ago. If a real catastrophe was imminent, wouldn't these countries have taken action before now?

Over 80% of the countries include offsets, such as sequestration, in their plans.[64]

Offsets are amorphous.

Here is a quotation from The Energy & Climate Intelligence Unit and Oxford Net-Zero report, *Taking Stock.*[65]

> Another concern is 'offsetting' through carbon credits — the practice of paying for emission cuts or carbon removal (often, by implication, in developing countries) rather than cutting emissions. Studies show that offsets do not always provide fully additional effort, and reliance on them may present risks to effective mitigation. And while nature-based offsetting is becoming increasingly popular, there are limits on the natural resources available: a recent Greenpeace report found that just two companies, Eni and International Airlines Group, could 'exhaust up to 12% of the available total' of carbon dioxide offsetting through new forests. Put simply; offsetting cannot be a substitute for significant emissions cuts.

The key points are:

> While nature-based offsetting is becoming increasingly popular, there are limits on the natural resources available.
>
> Put simply, offsetting cannot be a substitute for significant emissions cuts.

With respect to Surinam and Bhutan, these countries took no action except to claim that their forests will absorb all the CO2 their countries emit.

Some people may be confused by the claim that burning trees in place of coal in power plants won't affect CO2 emissions because the trees had already absorbed the CO2 being emitted.

There seems to be a contradiction between receiving credit for sequestering CO2 in trees and then being allowed to burn the trees without accounting for the CO2 being released.

Dozens of US corporations, together with many other organizations, have been swept into this climate caldron and established net-zero carbon goals.

The proposals for achieving net-zero carbon rely primarily on using wind and solar for generating electricity; on forests and underground sequestration to dispose of CO2; on battery-powered cars; and on desperate measures, such as long-term storage using batteries and hydrogen.

These unrealistic efforts ignore reality, where nearly 80% of the world's energy is derived from fossil fuels.

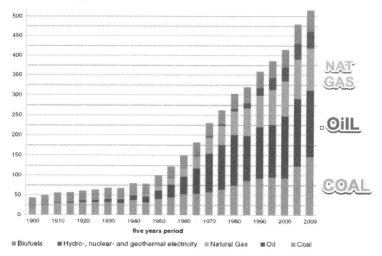

Figure 7, Energy Use in ExaJules.
Chart from *Climate Change Reconsidered II*,
Source: Bithas and Kalimares

In 2009, fossil fuel use was 82% of the total.

Since the publication of this graph, vast amounts of wind and solar have been added to the world's energy mix and now account for 3% of the mix. As a result, fossil fuels now account for 79% of the world's energy use.[66]

Over a ten-year period, billions have been spent on wind and solar, yet they remain only 3% of the world's energy mix.

This insignificant accomplishment illustrates the ineffectiveness of wind and solar, especially when considering that the electricity needed for BEVs and the heating of buildings must also be generated by wind and solar with a net-zero carbon policy.

With the use of battery-powered vehicles and electric heating of homes, US electricity usage is forecast to double by 2050.[67]

Germany has been very aggressive in its attempts to cut CO2 emissions. The Green party has driven the country to impose extreme measures, first with the Energiewende program to eliminate the use of fossil fuels in the generation of electricity, and now to convert all automobile manufacturing to battery-powered vehicles.

Energiewende has failed on two counts: The price of electricity has increased, not decreased, and the reduction in CO2 emissions has not been significantly greater than what the United States has achieved.

Germans pay three to four times as much for electricity as do Americans, and CO2 emissions have only been reduced by 22% since 2000.[68]

Germany spent billions promoting the use of wind and PV solar, with unimpressive results. By some accounts, Energiewende has been a failure.[69]

Based on the past ten years, it's reckless to expect wind and solar to replace fossil fuels with a doubling of electricity demand.

Yet, this is the foundation on which net-zero carbon is built.

Freedom is also at stake when it becomes clear that governments cannot achieve net-zero carbon without forcing people to reduce their carbon footprint.

The following example from the UK may have been extreme, but it was a genuine and frightening proposal.

Here is the quote from *The Daily Mail,* 16 November 2007, with the headline:

> *New green law could ration flights and raise fuel prices.*

The article went on to say:

> One method could be personal carbon-allowances, where everyone is given a fixed amount of carbon to use each year. Each time they travel in a plane, buy petrol, go shopping or eat out would be recorded on a plastic card. The more frugal could sell spare carbon to those who want to indulge themselves. But if you were to run out of your carbon allowance, you could be barred from flying or driving.

There were similar onerous proposals in HR2454, *The American Clean Energy and Security Act of 2009,* more commonly referred to as the Waxman-Markey Bill, that passed the House but failed in the Senate.

A section in HR2454 called for establishing efficiency standards for buildings, including homes, and then auditing the buildings to see whether they met the standards.

Meeting the standards would have been exceedingly expensive for older homes that weren't built with the wall space needed for extra insulation or that required new windows. With a public record of buildings failing to meet the standards, homes failing the audit would be hard to sell.

More recently, in 2020, the House passed the Moving Forward Act.

One section of interest is Sec. 90461, *Report on Greenhouse Gas Reporting Program.*

> The provision requires the Secretary of the Treasury to assess and report on the utility of the data from the Environmental Protection Agency's Greenhouse Gas Reporting Program for determining the amount of greenhouse gases emitted by each taxpayer for the purpose of imposing a fee on such taxpayers with respect to such emissions.

This would be a tax on every American, based on their greenhouse gas emissions.

Clearly, in its efforts to implement net-zero carbon policies, the government is striving to develop methods for enforcing them.

How many other ways will the government bureaucracy devise to control how you live? Or what you eat or where you travel?

Net-zero carbon policies are a threat to freedom.

Chapter 7

The Cabal

Who are behind the UNFCCC and the claim that CO2 emissions are a threat to mankind? Who are its supporters?

What are their motives?

We can begin with the former executive secretary of the UNFCCC, Christiana Figueres, who in 2015 said:

> This is probably the most difficult task we have ever given ourselves, which is to intentionally *transform the economic development model*, for the first time in human history. This is the first time in the history of mankind that we are setting ourselves the task of intentionally, within a defined period of time, to change the economic development model that has been reigning for the, at least, 150 years, since the industrial revolution.[70]

The world's economic model is based on capitalism.

Figueres made it clear it will be necessary to do away with capitalism to achieve the objective of cutting CO2 emissions.

Here is a quotation from Maurice Strong, the first Director of the United Nations Environmental Program (UNEP) and Director until 1975. In an interview, he describes how he would have a character in a novel ask:

> "Isn't the only hope for the planet that the industrialized civilization collapse? Isn't it our responsibility to bring it about?"[71]

In 1988, in combination with the World Meteorological Organization (WMO), UNEP established the Intergovernmental Panel on Climate Change (IPCC).

The IPCC is the go-to organization on climate issues for the UNFCCC.

Interestingly, the IPCC was never instructed to determine the cause of climate change, merely to assess human influence on climate, as stated in UNFCCC, Article 1.

UNFCCC, Article 1:

> Climate change means a change of climate which is attributed directly or indirectly to human activity that alters the composition of the global atmosphere and which is in addition to natural climate variability observed over comparable time periods.

The UNFCCC message? "Climate change is change attributable to human activity."

Ottmar Edenhofer, co-chair of the IPCC Working Group III, said in an interview by Neue Zurcher Zeitung (NZZ), November14, 2010:

> Climate policy has almost nothing to do anymore with environmental protection; the next world climate summit in Cancun is actually an economy summit during which the distribution of the world's resources will be negotiated.[72]

The IPCC has not always been truthful with the public when it issues its summary for policymakers (SPM). It's the SPM that is read by the media and politicians. The IPCC reports, themselves, are largely ignored by anyone but scientists.

Here is a glaring example of how the SPM misrepresents the IPCC reports.

In this example, evidence that could negate the CO2 hypothesis is excluded from the SPM.

Benjamin Santer, as lead author of Chapter 8, changed the 1995 SPM for Chapter 8.[73]

Original language as agreed to by the Chapter's authors:

> While some of the pattern-base discussed here have claimed detection of a significant climate change, *no study to date has positively attributed all or part of climate change observed to man-made causes.*

Revised language:

> The body of statistical evidence in chapter 8, when examined in the context of our physical understanding of the climate system, *now points to a discernible human influence on the global climate.*

Note that the revision claims there is a discernible human influence, while the original language said the opposite.

Throughout the literature, there is a common thread of Marxist ideology.

Dr. John Holdren, President Obama's senior advisor on science and technology, earlier in his career said:

> A transnational "Planetary Regime" should assume control of the global economy and also dictate the most intimate details of Americans' lives—using an armed international police force.[74]

Politiciens chimed in.

Former Senator Tim Wirth said, in 1993:

> We've got to ride the global warming issue. Even if the theory of global warming is wrong, we will be doing the right thing.[75]

Christine Stewart, Canada's former Minister of the Environment, was quoted by the *Calgary Herald* newspaper in 1998 as saying:

> No matter if the science is all phony, there are collateral environmental benefits. ... Climate change [provides] the greatest chance to bring about justice and equality in the world.[76]

And the popular culture includes quotes such as this from author Naomi Klein:

> Forget everything you think you know about global warming. The really inconvenient truth is that it's not about carbon—it's about capitalism.[77]

Those who favor net-zero carbon have attempted to disparage these quotations as being taken out of context. But at this point, the Marxist ideology is too pervasive to be ignored.

Words have meanings, and people tend to say what they mean.

Marxist ideology is built into the climate change movement.

Chapter 8

Modern Colonialism

For 400 years, European countries practiced colonialism, subjecting millions to be ruled by European masters.

Colonial empires died gradually, but all came to a decisive end after the Second World War.

A new colonialism is now underway, where underdeveloped countries are being subject to rules and regulations promoted most vigorously by institutions under the guise of the UNFCCC.

The World Bank, the International Monetary Fund (IMF), insurance and registration organizations, such as Swiss Re Group and DNV, financial institutions, such as Lazard, have all endorsed actions to eliminate the use of fossil fuels.

Underdeveloped countries pay the price of not using fossil fuels. And the price is continued poverty and death.

The UNFCCC and the Paris Agreement cajole underdeveloped countries to achieve net-zero carbon. Each is required to submit a national action plan, called Nationally Determined Contributions (NDCs).[78]

NDCs are not in the self-interest of developing countries that lack financial and other resources to abandon fossil fuels.

The Word Bank reported:

> About 800 million people live without electricity, and hundreds of millions have unreliable access. Almost 3 billion people still cook with biomass, such as wood, and with other fuels that cause severe air pollution, with widespread health impacts.[79]

Many of these people live in Africa, and this satellite image of Africa at night graphically depicts the plight of people living in Sub-Saharan Africa:

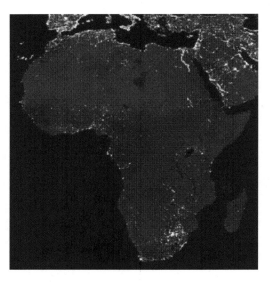

Figure 8, NASA satellite image of Africa at night.

The International Energy Agency (IEA) defines electricity access for use in its projections in this manner:

> Electricity access includes a household having an electricity supply connection, with a minimum level of consumption of 250 kilowatt-hours (kWh) per year for a rural household and 500 kWh for an urban household.

How does per capita electricity use in many Sub-Saharan countries compare with the IEA definition of electricity access?

All of the following countries fall below 250 kWh/year the level established for rural needs, let alone the needs of an urban household.

Table 4 Per Capita Electricity Consumption Sub-Saharan African Countries			
Country	kWh/ year	Country	kWh/ year
Chad	13	Burkina Faso	87
Guinea-Bissau	20	Democratic Republic of the Congo	99
Burundi	29	Tanzania	100
Central African Republic	30	Benin	101
Sierra Leon	31	Gambia	124
South Sudan	48	Entrea	127
Rwanda	61	Guinea	155
Niger	68	Mali	155
Liberia	70	Togo	155
Ethiopia	80	Kenya	166
Uganda	80	Mauritania	195
Malawi	81	Senegal	236

To put these numbers in perspective:

In Chad, one 60 watt light bulb could be used for slightly over 30 minutes daily.

In Senegal, two 60 watt light bulbs could be used for five and one-half hours daily.

The tragic truth is that 900 million people in Sub-Saharan Africa will use dung or wood for cooking their food, exposing families to terrible health problems and early death.[80]

Larger developing countries are also in need of electricity. Two of the largest are India and Indonesia (per capita consumption).

- India 935 kWh/year
- Indonesia 972 kWh/year

Indonesia has large coal reserves, which can allow it to develop inexpensive electricity using High Efficiency Low Emissions (HELE) coal-fired power plants.

India also has coal, which can allow it to also produce cheap electricity for its citizens.

Compare electricity usage of African countries, together with India, and Indonesia, with some of the European countries who are advocating for net-zero carbon.

Table 5 Per Capita Electricity Consumption European Countries			
Country	kWh/year	Country	kWh/year
Belgium	7,145	Germany	6,308
France	6,702	Denmark	5,620
The Netherlands	6,386	Italy	4,928

Here is the World Bank's position on funding coal-fired power plants.[81]

> The International Finance Corporation (IFC) and Multilateral Investment Guarantee Agency (MIGA) will apply three principles to investments across heavy manufacturing industries: First, they will not support new coal-fired power projects or wet process in cement.

and

> The IFC will no longer invest in the equity of financial intermediaries (FIs) that do not have a plan to phase out their investments in coal-related projects to zero or near-zero coal exposure by 2030.

Policies such as these will leave millions without adequate electricity.

Wind and solar are not the answer. They are unreliable and expensive. The electricity they generate is more expensive than electricity produced by coal-fired power plants.

Wind fails to generate electricity 65% of the time, while solar only generates electricity during daytime, or on average, 50% of the time, at best. Wind and solar need back up, and this means using expensive batteries if natural gas is disallowed by net-zero carbon policies.

Poor countries are in no position to produce or import hydrogen, the proposed alternative to natural gas. Moreover, producing hydrogen requires electricity, which these countries already lack.

Without coal or natural gas, these countries are trapped in poverty that kills.

The disadvantages of wind and solar are set forth in Chapter 2.

At the June 2021 G7 meeting, the G7 leaders pledged to reach net-zero carbon emissions by 2050.[82]

The United States should not participate in these net-zero carbon policies that reek of colonialism.

Chapter 9

Economic War

Europe is proposing to declare economic war on the United States.

While this may or may not come to pass, it's important to consider how an economic war would affect the United States.

The EU is proposing to establish CO2 mandates on imports, making US products expensive and potentially preventing them from being sold in European countries, unless the United States also adopts net-zero carbon policies.

The EU mandate will be called a carbon border adjustment mechanism (CBAM).

Quoting from a CLEW fact sheet:[83]

> Simply put, such a levy would add the same CO2 costs to a product when it crosses the border into the EU that the manufacturer of a domestically produced item would have to pay.

The CBAM plan will create a new bureaucracy, i.e., agency, to monitor the carbon content of imported goods. Anyone importing goods into the EU would need to register with the EU's new agency and audit the carbon content of their suppliers.

The EU's rationale for imposing these CO2 restrictions is to prevent carbon leakage, where EU manufacturers produce products, normally built in Europe, in other countries, such as Asia, for importation into Europe.

Why would the EU impose such restrictions on imports?

The EU's stated rationale for imposing these CO2 restrictions is to prevent carbon leakage.

The more important unstated reason for the CBAM regulation is that the EU has created an economic nightmare for European countries that depend on exports for employment and economic growth.

This risk is clearly noted in the CLEW fact sheet, which lists "Distorting trade and damaging EU industry" as a concern.

Recent new EU regulations have stiffened requirements for reducing CO2 emissions. The EU now requires that greenhouse-gas emissions be cut 55% by 2030 compared with 1990, and then achieve net-zero carbon emissions by 2050.

These regulations are having a perverse effect on EU countries.

Regulations to eliminate fossil fuels are creating an environment where the products EU countries produce will be uncompetitive on the world market.

Electricity is already expensive, except that industries have been granted special low rates for the electricity they use.

In addition, industries are given special allowances to offset the higher cost of electricity. Quoting a CLEW fact sheet:

> Under the EU Emissions Trading Scheme (ETS), free emission rights are given to energy-intensive companies that meet product-related benchmarks and are at risk of carbon leakage. In addition, member states are permitted to return some of the ETS revenue to electricity-intensive businesses.

With increasingly stringent regulations on CO2 emissions, industries, such as steel and cement, will see their costs skyrocket as they try to use hydrogen to replace natural gas or rely on carbon capture and sequestration to eliminate CO2 emissions.

Transportation costs will also increase with the imposition of battery and hydrogen fuel-cell-powered vehicles.

The high cost of steel and cement, and other products, such as aluminum, will permeate manufacturers' supply chains.

With high costs for their materials and transportation, all EU countries will find their products, from automobiles to wine, uncompetitive on the world market.

Germany, for example, depends on exports, and net-zero carbon policies will kill the export market for German goods.

One obstacle to the CBAM is the need to comply with World Trade Organization (WTO) rules.

Turning again to the CLEW fact sheet:

> The WTO's free trade principle of "non-discrimination" by which the European Union must abide [under GATT], would be breached if the bloc differentiated between low and high-carbon products that are otherwise alike.

> The GATT provides for exceptions to this rule for environmental reasons, but the CBAM would have to be designed to exactly meet the requirements. Jennifer A. Hillman, a senior fellow at the Council on Foreign Relations, a nonprofit think tank, told Reuters the EU could strengthen its case by ensuring that revenue from the mechanism goes to climate action.

Already we can see how US sympathizers are trying to assist the EU in establishing net-zero carbon policies.

Here is a quotation from an earlier paper by Jennifer Hillman, who was commenting on a proposed US law establishing a border tax.[84]

The key is to structure any accompanying border measure as a straightforward extension of the domestic climate policy to imports. If so designed, there should be few questions about the measure's consistency with the WTO rules.

In other words, the WTO will probably not stand in the way of the EU establishing the CBAM if it decides to do so.

It's also clear that one of the purposes of the proposed CBAM is to force other countries to adopt net-zero carbon policies.

For example, EU Commission president Ursula von der Leyen said,[85]

This Carbon Border Adjustment Mechanism should motivate foreign producers and EU importers to reduce their carbon emissions, while ensuring that we level the playing field in a WTO-compatible way.

Other organizations and individuals who support net-zero carbon regulations in the United States also support the EU's proposed CBAM.

Some raise concerns that the United States won't be able to sell into European markets. For example, Senator Bill Cassidy of Louisiana said, "We will lose the European Union as a market."[86]

This flies in the face of the facts.

The EU has created policies that result in European products being uncompetitive on the world market.

As noted, the CBAM is an effort to force the United States and other countries to adopt net-zero carbon policies.

Products made in the United States are of the high quality most countries would be delighted to purchase, and with the CBAM, products made in the US will be less expensive than products made in Europe.

The United States can increase market share in the Mideast, Africa, South East Asia, and South America. Europeans will still buy US products, even with the CO2 penalty, when they are better than products made in Europe.

The United States holds the stronger hand unless it arbitrarily relinquishes it by adopting net-zero carbon policies.

By now, it should be clear that adopting net-zero carbon policies will weaken the United States and harm all Americans.

Part 3
Realities

Each one hopes that if he feeds the crocodile enough, the crocodile will eat him last. All of them hope that the storm will pass before their turn comes to be devoured. But I fear greatly that the storm will not pass. It will rage and it will roar ever more loudly, ever more widely.

Winston Churchill, 1940

Chapter 10

Climate Science

This chapter describes the facts and data that lead to the conclusion CO2 emissions are not an existential threat to mankind.

My previous book, *The Looming Energy Crisis*, listed over 40 scientists acknowledged as climate scientists. The list included an IPCC reviewer and a Nobel Laureate.

It also lists over 60 scientists from multiple disciplines, who are successful climate scientists. Climate science is a multi-discipline science.

It also referenced the team of scientists and astronauts who put a man on the moon and who have, as a group, determined that CO2 emissions are not an existential threat to mankind.

It also identified many additional well-qualified scientists who signed a petition saying, "There is no convincing evidence that human release of CO2 will cause a disruption to the Earth's climate."

With hundreds of qualified scientists saying, on the record, that CO2 is not a threat, any notion that 97% of scientists believe CO2 is an existential threat to mankind is bogus.

What are the facts that can lead anyone to reach the same conclusion that CO2 is not a threat?

We can begin with the fact there have been several periods over the last 10,000 years, known as the Holocene, where temperatures have been higher than today and where CO2 levels were flat, at approximately 280 ppm.

The cause of these higher temperatures has been debated, but there is little question they occurred.

We can turn next to the 1859 Carrington Event. This unusual and powerful magnetic storm from the sun enveloped the Earth, causing considerable consternation among observers and significant damage to telegraph systems.

In one instance, a telegraph operator was struck in the forehead by an arc that leaped from the equipment as the aurora created a strong, steady flow of current in the wires. In another, two operators disconnected the batteries and operated the telegraph using only the current produced by the aurora.

The Carrington Event is described in detail in the book, *The Sun Kings* by Stuart Clark.

The Carrington Event was well documented.

More recently, in 1989, a geomagnetic storm, one-third the size of the Carrington Event, caused power transformers in Quebec, Canada, to fail.

The threat of solar storms is recognized by Congress.[87]

It's clear: The sun can reach out and affect the earth. This is something every meteorologist already knows.

It is widely believed the Little Ice Age resulted from a lack of sunspots for nearly seventy-five years, a period known as the Maunder Minimum.

Figure 9 shows the sunspot cycles from 1610 to 2010.

An astronomer, the first person who identified a linkage between sunspots and the earth, was William Herschel (1738-1822).

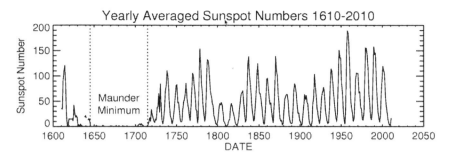

Figure 9, Sunspots 1610-2010, Graph from NASA

Herschel had previously shown that invisible rays from the sun produced higher temperatures during his experiments, comparing temperatures with colors produced by a prism.[88]

He had discovered infrared heat emanating from the sun.

But this led him to explore the relationship between the price of wheat and the number of sunspots. Comparing his record of sunspots going back decades with the price of wheat during the same period, he found that the price of wheat rose when there were few sunspots and went down when there were more sunspots.

This demonstrated that sunspots affected the earth's climate.

The mechanism of how the sun affected the earth's climate wasn't established with any certainty until the late 1990s when Henrik Svensmark of the Danish National Space Institute proposed that the sun could affect the number of cosmic rays entering the earth's atmosphere. He hypothesized that cosmic rays could affect cloud cover, and as a result, affect temperatures.

The debate surrounding the Svensmark hypothesis led to an experiment at the CERN research center.

The CERN research center in Europe derived its name from the French "Conseil Européen pour la Recherche Nucléaire," or European Council for Nuclear Research.

This premier research center conducted an experiment to determine whether cosmic rays could form clouds and the conditions under which cloud formation would occur.

The results of the CLOUD experiment established two facts.

- The first put an end to the long-held belief that there were fewer clouds before the industrial revolution.

- The second proved cosmic rays could form clouds.

It was learned from the experiment that hydrocarbons released by plants could provide the necessary conditions for cloud formation and that sulfuric acid aerosols were not needed.

Here is a quotation from a summary report:

> [The scientists] introduced a mixture of natural oxidants present in the air and an organic hydrocarbon released by coniferous plants. The hydrocarbon was rapidly oxidized. The only other ingredient allowed in the chamber was cosmic rays, high energy radiation from outer space, which made the molecules clump together into aerosols. Sulfuric acid was not required. In fact, even when the researchers introduced low concentrations of sulfuric acid to the chamber such as might be found in unpolluted air, the aerosol formation rate was unaffected. In a second CLOUD experiment published simultaneously in Nature, researchers showed these same oxidized molecules could rapidly grow the particles to sizes big enough to seed cloud droplets.

Nevertheless, there is still a debate over whether cosmic rays can affect cloud formation.

The formation of low-level clouds can affect temperatures by reflecting solar radiation back to space, so the Svensmark hypothesis can be an important piece of the puzzle.

The IPCC has published the results of computer programs that are the basis for much of the fear concerning CO2 emissions and their effect on climate.

Media reports have used the IPCC's RCP 8.5 scenario to predict climate catastrophes.

Much of the fear of catastrophic outcomes are based on RCP 8.5, (RCP = representative concentration pathway).[89]

The IPCC uses scenarios, i.e., hypothetical events with accompanying data programmed into computers, to demonstrate the scenario's effect on temperatures.

Scientists have pointed out that RCP 8.5 is an extreme case, and is not supported by known facts.

Forbes, in an article by Pielke, said this about RCP 8.5:[90]

> It's Time To Get Real
> About The Extreme Scenario
> Used To Generate Climate Porn

> The misuse of RCP 8.5 is endemic. In fact, if you see a news story with dramatic projections of future climate impacts, you should expect that it comes from RCP 8.5.

Nevertheless, the media and proponents of catastrophic climate change continue to reference RCP 8.5 as business as usual, which has resulted in the public being bombarded with misinformation.

In addition, the computer programs published by the IPCC do not reflect what is actually happening to temperatures on the earth.

Dr. John Christy, in his Congressional testimony, used the following chart, Figure 10, to demonstrate that the IPCC computer projections were overstating temperature rise.[91]

Figure 10 shows that the average of 102 computer programs projected a temperature rise that was more than twice the actual temperature readings taken by satellites and balloons.

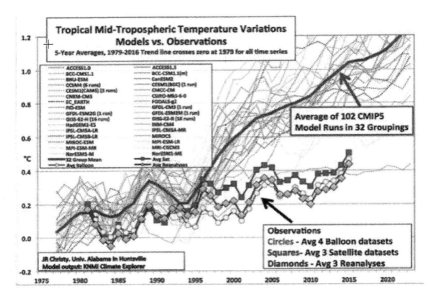

Figure 10, Dr. John Christy Congressional Testimony
Comparison of actual temperatures vs. computer projections

He also showed, in Figure 11, that when IPCC computer models omitted greenhouse gas data, the program results came closer to corresponding to actual temperature readings, thus casting additional doubt about IPCC projections.

Quoting Dr. Christy:

> What is immediately evident is that the model trends in which extra GHGs are included lie completely outside of the range of the observational trends, indicating again that the models, as hypotheses, failed a simple "scientific-method" test applied to this fundamental, climate-change variable.

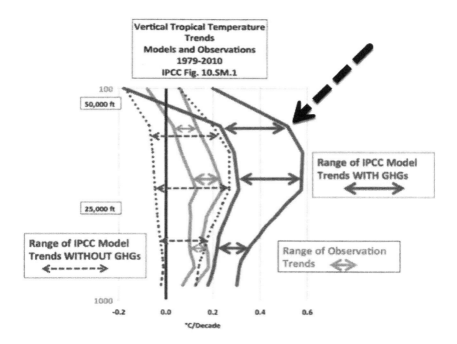

Figure 11, Dr. John Christy Congressional Testimony
Model trends with and without GHGs

In other words, when GHG data (solid dark gray lines) is omitted from the program, the computer output (dotted lines) aligns with actual temperatures (solid light gray lines). Therefore, GHG data is distorting the outcomes. Solid vertical line denotes 0 degrees C per decade.

The heavy dotted arrow, superimposed on Dr. Christy's chart, points to when the GHG data is included in the program, which is when the program output is far removed from the actual readings.

Another climate scientist, Dr. Judith Curry, in 2017, said:

> There is growing evidence that climate models are running too hot and that climate sensitivity to carbon dioxide is at the lower end of the range provided by the IPCC.

This establishes that computer programs used to support the narrative that CO2 is a threat are wrong. Their output shows warming that is at least two to three times greater than what is actually occurring.

Note also that the warming detected by balloons and satellites could be from natural causes rather than from increased levels of CO2 in the atmosphere.

This is an important distinction.

Then in 2020, Dr. Judith Curry drew three main conclusions from her latest paper, *Plausible scenarios for climate change: 2020-2050*.

She said,

1. We are starting to narrow the uncertainty in the amount of warming from emissions that we can expect out to 2050.

2. All three modes of natural variability — solar, volcanoes, internal variability — are expected to trend cool over the next three decades.

3. Depending on the relative magnitudes of emissions driven warming versus natural variability, decades with no warming or even cooling are more or less plausible.

The accompanying table from Dr. Curry's paper shows the possibility of cooler temperatures.

Table 6			
	Warmest	**Moderate**	**Coldest**
Emisions	0.70	0.52	0.35
Volcanoes	0	-0.11	-0.30
Solar	0	-0.10	-0.25
Oceans	0	-0.20	-0.30
NET	0.70	0.11	-0.50

Table 6, From *Plausible scenarios for climate change: 2020-2050* by Dr. J. Curry

This suggests the possibility of cooling temperatures.

Another scientist, Dr. William Happer, has provided evidence that increased levels of atmospheric CO2, and other greenhouse gases, such as methane, will not cause a dangerous increase in temperatures.[92]

The next graph establishes that a doubling of atmospheric CO2 will have a negligible effect on temperatures. There is a similar graph for methane, etc.

The circled area highlights the essential information used to reach conclusions about the effect of doubling atmospheric levels of CO2.

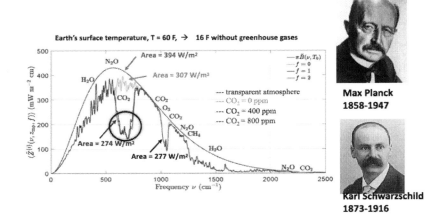

Figure 12, Graph from Dr. Happer's
Hillsdale College presentation.[93]

The top solid curve, was developed by Max Planck. It establishes the thermal heat loss at various wavelengths as if there was no atmosphere.

Quoting Dr. Happer:

> The area under the solid curve is how much heat radiation would be emitted to space from each square meter of Earth's surface, at a mean temperature of 15.5 C.

The lower, jagged curve was developed by Karl Schwarzschild. Schwarzschild's curve shows the actual thermal heat loss from the Earth as radiation is interrupted at various wavelengths by components of the atmosphere; in this particular instance, the effect of CO2.

The graph shows the heat loss where the percentages of CO2 are:
- 0 ppm, (very light grey, jagged curve),
- 400 ppm (black, jagged curve)
- 800 ppm (light grey, within the circle).

These two curves, where circled, are virtually the same, indicating that heat loss is nearly unchanged after doubling CO2 from 400 to 800 ppm.

Dr. Happer also provided text used in his Hillsdale presentation, which sheds light on the era in which Dr. Planck worked.

> Max Planck remained in Germany during another crusade, the Nazi hijacking of German culture. Planck did his best to protect Jewish scientists who were targets of Nazi hatred. He paid a heavy price for his courage. His son, Erwin Planck, was hung by the Nazis in January, 1945, for alleged involvement in a plot to assassinate Hitler.

What can we conclude from the above information?

Here is a summary of the facts.

- We know it has been warmer than today, several times over the past 10,000 years.

- We also know that the sun can affect conditions on the earth, possibly dramatically.

- We have some reason to believe that cosmic rays act to modulate the effect of the sun's solar activity on the earth.

- We know that the IPCC computer projections overstate the actual temperature rise by two to three times.

- There is also scientific evidence that a doubling of CO2, or other greenhouse gasses, will not significantly affect temperatures.

These facts establish the rationale for concluding that, even if CO2 leads to some warming, CO2 emissions will not result in catastrophic events.

Net-zero carbon policies are not needed to protect mankind from climate change, and will have disastrous consequences for the United States.

Chapter 11

Ramifications of Net-zero Carbon

How will attempting to achieve net-zero carbon affect the United States?

Will the consequences be minor and easily overlooked or overcome?

Or will they be catastrophic?

Power Generation

The primary consequences of attempting to achieve net-zero carbon for power generation and operation of the grid are two-fold.

- Cost
- Blackouts

It's very likely that net-zero carbon policies will result in a doubling or tripling of the cost of electricity.

Germany, which has studiously pursued a policy of cutting CO_2 emissions, charges Germans two to three times more for electricity than the average American pays.

California which has pursued a net-zero policy charges 23.4 cents per kWh while the average cost for other Americans is 13.8 cents per kWh.[94]

The people hurt the most by net-zero carbon policies, and the resulting high cost of electricity, are the poorest among us, who can least afford the higher cost.

While higher electricity prices harm the economy and hurt the poor, blackouts are the greatest threat stemming from net-zero carbon policies.

The February, 2021, Texas blackouts killed 210 people, though some claim the toll was much higher.[95]

The disaster could have been far greater, with the Texas grid coming within minutes of total collapse. A total collapse would have required a black start, which could have taken weeks before the grid had been restored.

A blackout not only turns off the lights, it shuts down services.

Anything powered by electricity will stop running.

Water supplies will shut down due to a lack of electric pumps when gravity flow is exhausted. Refrigeration is shut down, destroying food supplies in homes and stores. Gasoline pumps won't work, eliminating transportation as cars and trucks run out of fuel. Battery powered vehicles won't be able to recharge their batteries. Heating and air-conditioning won't work. Elevators in big cities will fail, trapping people inside until they can be rescued.

In Texas, people were only without electricity for an average of 42 hours. What if it had been for a week? Or a month?

We know this is within the realm of possibility. We have it on record that wind and solar were unable to supply electricity for 14 days in New England.[96] Secretary of Energy Moniz reported there had been a period of nine days in Texas where the wind hadn't blown.[97]

When it comes to the reliability of the grid, we can't be almost sure, we must be absolutely certain that blackouts of long duration can't occur.

Net-zero carbon policies leave Americans in great danger of catastrophic blackouts.

Transportation

Battery powered vehicles (BEVs) are the policy prescription for eliminating fossil fuels from the majority of the transportation sector.

How will eliminating the sale of internal combustion engine (ICE) vehicles by 2050 affect the United States?

According to the International Energy Agency (IEA), the United States is the world leader in extracting and processing oil and natural gas.

Table 7 shows the three leading countries in the extraction and processing of oil and natural gas. (This data is before the United States government's actions in 2020 to curtail pipelines and oil and gas development.)

Table 7 Fossil Fuel Sources		
Fossil Fuel	**Extraction - Country (%)**	**Refining - Country (%)**
Oil	**United States (18),** Saudi Arabia (17), Russia (7)	**United States (20),** China (17), Russia (7)
		LNG Export - Country (%)
Natural Gas	**United States (24),** Russia (18), Iran (8)	**Qatar (21),** Australia (21), United States (10)
Note: % = Approximate percentage of world supply, with largest in boldface.		

A net-zero carbon policy will transform the United States from being the world's leader in energy, to being beholden to others for the materials needed to manufacture battery powered vehicles.

And most significantly, the United States becomes beholden to China, its fiercest competitor on the world stage.

As seen from Table 3, page 32, China is the predominant supplier of critical battery materials.

Not to be overlooked, wind turbines are also dependent on China for critical materials.

Wind turbines rely heavily on rare earths, and China provides over 80% of these materials.

Wind turbines also rely on zinc. While the United States does produce some zinc, China supplies 34% of the world's supply.[98]

<u>Industry and Technology</u>

The United States is the technology leader in the following major industries.

- Jet engines
- Natural gas power plants
- Oil exploration and production
- Natural gas exploration and production
- Low cost, reliable electricity
- Equipment for the Armed Forces
- Mining equipment

The United States, at a minimum, has technology equal to others in these major industries:

- LNG exports
- Airplane design and manufacturing
- Automobile design and manufacturing
- Chip design and manufacturing
- Pharma

- Nuclear power
- Communications

The United States is a laggard in the following important industries.

- Battery manufacturing
- Mining

All of the industries in which the United States has technology leadership are dependent on fossil fuels, except, possibly, mining equipment.

With the elimination of fossil fuels, the United States industry and technology leadership will become irrelevant, or of vastly diminished importance.

Battery manufacturing and mining, industries in which the United States lags, will be the most important with the adoption of net-zero carbon.

While not immediately obvious, the United States, a major manufacturing country, has some of the lowest cost energy and most reliable electricity in the world, essential for chip manufacturing, which is an important competitive advantage that will disappear with net-zero policies.

American companies eager to join the Paris Agreement bandwagon or that have established net-zero carbon goals stand to be devoured by the crocodile.

The Chief Executive of Dow Chemical, who had supported rejoining the Paris Agreement, went to the White House to plead on behalf of natural gas.

Quoting the Wall Street Journal: "He warned about the potential consequences of any policy that would exclude natural gas from the energy mix."

He now realizes that net-zero carbon will cost his company dearly after investing billions in factories to take advantage of America's abundant, cheap natural gas.

CEOs who have benefited from acquiescing to the government's climate policies will now have to confront the crocodile.

A few countries may have low cost energy, but lack manufacturing prowess. A good example is Norway, which has low cost electricity from hydro and cheap oil from the North Sea, but lacks broad manufacturing capabilities because of its small population.

Equipment for the Armed Forces, as an industry, relies heavily on fossil fuels, e.g., diesel, gasoline and jet fuel. Fossil fuels are essential for the safe and effective operation of a wide variety of equipment, including, tanks, ships, and aircraft.

Biofuels cannot replace these fuels. There are insufficient source materials, such as grease, garbage, and trees, or algae, to produce sufficient quantities of biofuels for aircraft or diesel engines.[99]

In addition, the infrastructure to deliver bio-fuels to America's Armed Forces operating in multiple locations, thousands of miles from the continental United States, does not exist. These fuels must be delivered by oilers, to foreign bases, or, in the case of the Navy, to other ships using underway replenishment.

Net-zero carbon has the United States trade energy independence for dependence on other countries for materials.

Conclusions

On Marxism:

The entire ideology is built on a fairy tale, yet delivers a nightmare of horrors.

Mark Levin, *American Marxism*

Chapter 12

Conclusions

Net-zero carbon policies are based on fear and panic.

Panic leads to bad decisions.

Panic precludes allowing science and technology to meet whatever challenges we face.

If BEVs are the preferred choice of the average citizen, science and technology will strive, over time, to develop batteries that are superior to lithium-ion batteries and that don't require the use of scarce and hard to extract minerals. For example, the aluminum-air battery might be the answer if science has the time needed to develop it.

The development of micro-nuclear power plants could provide power where it is needed while also improving grid reliability.

In nearly every instance, net-zero carbon policies increase costs and reduces reliability or quality, while in a few instances, they only increase costs. It's difficult to identify any net-zero policy that improves anything.

There is no need to panic, because climate change is not an existential threat.

We can live in freedom, without fear, and allow science and technology and a free market economy to meet whatever challenges we face.

This is the American way.

Mark Levin's comments on Marxism at the beginning of this section apply equally well to net-zero carbon.

> The entire ideology is built on a fairy tale, yet delivers a nightmare of horrors.[100]

The ramifications of net-zero carbon can be summarized in two sentences.

Net-zero carbon means greater risks for Americans, and an enfeebling of the United States on the world stage.

The major beneficiary of America's decline will be America's enemies, especially China.

Appendix A

Carbon Capture and Sequestration

As mentioned in Chapter 1, the theoretical processes to effect removal of CO_2 from the atmosphere, or for preventing it from reaching the atmosphere, can be grouped as follows.

- Capturing CO_2 from where it is produced, i.e., carbon capture
- Using CO_2 in the process, such as in the making of steel
- Sequestering CO_2 underground
- Sequestering CO_2 in plant growth
- Geoengineering, such as fertilizing the oceans to increase plankton growth to absorb CO_2 from the atmosphere

Each of these is either unproven or has serious limitations.

Carbon Capture and Sequestration (CCS) is a multistep process with hurdles at each step.

The CO_2 must first be captured, then compressed to around 2,200 psi for transport in pipelines, and then injected underground into a geologic formation.

There are three methods for capturing CO_2.
- Pre combustion
- Oxyfuel combustion
- Post-combustion

These were originally designed for use with coal-fired power plants and are being adapted for use in industrial processes.

Pre-combustion is the most difficult. It uses a gasifier to turn coal into a synthetic gas, allowing the CO_2 and hydrogen to be separated from the syngas stream. Then the hydrogen is burned while the CO_2 is compressed and piped away for sequestration underground.

Oxyfuel combustion is when the fuel is burned in a pure oxygen environment, which results in pure CO_2 and water with the CO_2 easy to capture. Oxygen is separated from the air and then piped to the boiler's firebox, i.e., combustion chamber, where it is burned with the fuel, usually coal. As a result the exhaust gas has a high concentration of CO_2.

Post-combustion uses solvents to absorb the CO_2 from the exhaust stream and then releases the captured CO_2 by heating the solvent.

Post-combustion has been used with coal-fired and NGCC power plants, but the plants must be derated because a large portion of the power plant's output is used to capture, compress, and transport CO_2.

Capturing CO_2 from an NGCC power plant results in a derating of the plant by around 30%, requiring the building of additional generating capacity to replace the power lost in capturing, compressing, and transporting the liquid CO_2 to where it can be sequestered underground.

A 900 MW, NGCC power plant becomes a 600 MW power plant, with the need to build 300 MW of new capacity to replace the power lost by CCS.

Sequestration is the third step.

There have been many demonstration projects for sequestering CO_2, with the Sleipner CO_2 storage facility offshore Norway probably the best known. As of today, it has stored approximately 19 million tons of CO_2 underground or 0.85 tons per year.[101]

Most other projects have used the captured CO2 for enhanced oil recovery (EOR). But, obviously, with the winding down of the oil industry with net-zero carbon, EOR won't be very useful.

With net-zero carbon, CCS will be essential for use in those situations where CO2 emissions can't be prevented, such as in the steel and cement industries. Sequestering CO2 in forests and plants, as part of Nationally Determined Contribution (NDC) action plans by countries complying with UNFCCC requirements, is assumed to be legitimate.

Captured CO2 from an industrial process, such as a steel mill, is first converted to a liquid by compressing it to around 2,200 psi for transport to where it can be injected underground.

This will require building pipelines since most steel mills, etc., aren't built over locations where CO2 can be sequestered underground.

There are safety issues with CO2 pipelines operating at over 2,000 psi.

CO2, as a gas, is odorless and heavier than air, and if it leaks from a pipeline, it can settle undetected into low-lying areas, which, if occupied, can cause death.

The ultimate question concerning sequestration is whether the CO2 will remain trapped underground for thousands of years or will it leak back into the atmosphere.

Only two Class VI wells have been approved for sequestering CO2 underground in the United States, primarily because of the risks involved.

While some CO2 has been sequestered underground for thirty years or so, there have been examples of where the geologic storage of natural gas was considered safe, yet leaks occurred.

- Aliso Canyon, California

The leak was discovered on October 23, 2015. It required over four thousand people in a nearby community to move to temporary quarters. Senators Boxer and Feinstein immediately declared the need for a federal investigation, similar to the Macondo investigation, to determine whether the nationwide network of 400 natural gas storage sites are safe.[102]

- Hutchinson, Kansas

The explosion from the leak occurred on January 17, 2001. The leak was determined to have come from underground geologic storage of natural gas in a layer of salt called the Hutchinson Salt Member of the Wellington Formation.[103]

Another leak from an above-ground valve shows that the piping and control of underground storage are also critical.

- Liberty County, Texas

A storage facility in Liberty County, Texas, 16 miles north of Houston, had a well control incident and natural gas fire that took over six days to extinguish in 2004. The incident was caused by a valve controlling the salt dome storage facility.[104]

Notes

1. EPA report on CO2 emissions https://bit.ly/3B4BKTt

2. EPA reported CO2 emissions in 2004 of 5,988 MMT https://bit.ly/3y6kYBe

3. German GHG emissions https://bit.ly/3khh049

4. US CO2 emission reductions https://bit.ly/2Wd6EK2

5. China to cap emissions https://reut.rs/3z8x6mP

6. China CO2 emissions 2004 https://go.nature.com/3sCRXMk

7. China CO2 emissions in 2019 https://bit.ly/3j7Etp4

8. India CO2 emissions https://bit.ly/3sByrQn

9. The Wall Street Journal, August 10, 2021 *A Climate Catastrophe*

10. China's coal usage https://bit.ly/3glwpz6

11. China new coal-fired power plants https://bit.ly/2Uzz5Bq

12. Ditto

13. CO2 emissions major countries https://bit.ly/3fM4QMi

14. *The Hundred-Year Marathon,* by Michael Pillsbury, ISBN 978-1-62779-010-9

15. Ditto

16. UK Gov statement re Hong Kong https://bit.ly/3AYs90i

17. White House Fact Sheet https://bit.ly/2WKY6KJ

18. UN website https://bit.ly/3kabobL

19. Class VI, EPA https://bit.ly/38h5Jv7

20. Competitive Enterprise Institute, WUWT, 4/9/21 https://bit.ly/2Ro4gxM

21. Aliso Canyon https://bit.ly/3sD5eET

22. Hutchinson, KS https://bit.ly/3AZ0yfj

23. IPCC Global Warming 1.5° C https://bit.ly/3j6g96Y

24. Moniz, The Washington Post Live, March 31, 2021 https://wapo.st/3uDgC3q

25. Wall Street Journal, *Start Up Claims Battery Breakthrough*, R. Gold, July 23, 2021

26. Special Report, *Green Nightmare for Americans*, https://bit.ly/33ekRH7

27. *The Looming Energy Crisis, Are Blackouts Inevitable?* by D. Dears, 978-0-9815119-9-3

28. ERCOT News Release Dec 16, 2020 https://bit.ly/2Wc4fPZ

29. Figure 8, NRG Fourth Quarter and Full Year 2018 Earning Presentation https://bit.ly/3j48kOR

30. California diverts hydropower https://bit.ly/3glnT37

31. *The Looming Energy Crisis, Are Blackouts Inevitable?* by D. Dears, 978-0-9815119-9-3

32. From ISO-NE cold weather operations report December 24, 2017, to January 8, 2018 http://bit.ly/2q7Eldb

33. *Shorting the Grid*, by Meredith Angwin ISBN 978-1-7353580-0-0

34. Article, September, 2017, *Misleading Costs for Wind and Solar* https://bit.ly/2V14b52

35. *The Levelized Cost of Electricity from Existing Generation Resources*, The Institute of Energy Research https://bit.ly/2UjCPqQ

36. NREL Electrification Futures Study, 2021 https://bit.ly/3s8HNl6

37. Special Report, *Green Nightmare for Americans* https://bit.ly/33ekRH7

38. Hydrogen and Climate Change at https://bit.ly/3wgJOP3

39. Chapter 10, *Nothing to Fear*, by Donn Dears, ISBN 978-0-9815119-2-4

40. GM announcement https://bit.ly/2UHmM6k

41. *The Role of Critical Minerals*, IEA, Page 13 https://bit.ly/3j44KEr

42. Reuters, Native American Tribe https://reut.rs/383kCks

43. *The Role of Critical Minerals*, IEA, Page 6 https://bit.ly/3j44KEr

44. GM Lordstown plant https://bit.ly/2Wh5XPK

45. Ditto

46. Charging station costs https://bit.ly/3y7Co0y

47. Steel and cement CO2 emissions https://bit.ly/2XFGH6x

48. Special report, *Hydrogen and Climate Change* https://bit.ly/3wgJOP3

49. EU Hydrogen strategy https://bit.ly/3kcF6wT

50. EU hydrogen pipeline map https://bit.ly/2TDRwRN

51. M. Ball, M. Weeda, *Compendium of Hydrogen Energy* https://bit.ly/3vOtZyg

52. Ditto

53. Energy Information Agency https://bit.ly/3y63E0r

54. NREL, Cost Estimate Using Water Hydrolysis https://bit.ly/3uPOc5R

55. EIA, natural gas pipelines network https://bit.ly/3fewAL0

56. EIA, https://bit.ly/3glbtID

57. NREL, *Blending Hydrogen*, pipeline report https://bit.ly/3fbvmAf

58. Argonne National Laboratory https://bit.ly/33GEcRp

59. Chapter 1, *Nothing to Fear*, by Donn Dears, ISBN 978-0-9815119-2-4

60. UN Climate Action https://bit.ly/3kabobL

61. UNFCCC Bhutan Reports https://bit.ly/3D7e3LV

62. UNFCCC Surinam https://bit.ly/2XN4B07

63. UN Energy & Climate Intelligence Unit https://bit.ly/384EX8S

64. *Taking Stock*, Figure 5 https://bit.ly/3DgSg4G

65. Ditto

66. World's energy mix https://bit.ly/37ZG5e0

67. NREL Electrification Futures Study, 2021 https://bit.ly/3s8HNl6

68. Clean Energy Wire https://bit.ly/3khh049

69. IEEE Spectrum https://bit.ly/37Z9ViV

70. Figueres quote https://bit.ly/3j6cPsh

71. Maurice Strong quote https://bit.ly/2WimAuM

72. Ottmar Edenhofer quote http://bit.ly/2I35kRG

73. Page 64, *Human Caused Global Warming*, by Dr. Tim Ball

74. Dr. John Holdren quotation, *Human Caused Global Warming*, by Dr. Tim Ball

75. Tim Wirth quotation https://bit.ly/3mlS4e9

76. Cristine Stewart quote https://bit.ly/3jc7hNf

77. Naomi Klein quotation, *This Changes Everything*, by Naomi Klein

78. UN Climate Action https://bit.ly/3kabob

79. World Bank climate action plan https://bit.ly/3D3LaAh

80. Sub-Saharan cooking fuel https://bit.ly/384ODjY

81. World Bank climate action plan https://bit.ly/3D3LaAh

82. G7 Communique https://bit.ly/3gly4Vn

83. CLEW CABM Fact sheet https://bit.ly/3860xtP

84. J Hillman paper on GATT and WTO https://bit.ly/3y6kGKI

85. EU President Ursula von der Leyen https://bit.ly/3j6rzYo

86. Senator Cassidy https://bit.ly/3iyevL6

87. Solar flares and wind https://bit.ly/3j7DYve

88. *The Sun Kings* by Stuart Clark ISBN 978-0-691-12660-9

89. RCP 8.5 https://bit.ly/37Z4lwW

90. Pielke on RCP 8.5 https://bit.ly/3kfi6gI

91. Christy Congressional Testimony https://bit.ly/3AZcnlH

92. W. A. van Wijngaarden and W. Happer paper https://bit.ly/3mpTNwh

93. *How to Think About Climate Change*, Hillsdale College, February 19, 2021

94. California electricity cost https://bit.ly/3kbcXWN

95. Texas blackout deaths https://bit.ly/3D9AArk

96. From ISO-NE cold weather operations report December 24, 2017, to January 8, 2018 http://bit.ly/2q7Eldb

97. Moniz, The Washington Post Live, March 31, 2021 https://wapo.st/3uDgC3q

98. Zinc supplies https://bit.ly/3D9AXSK

99. *Nothing to Fear*, Chapter 10, ISBN 978-0-9815119-2-4

100. Mark Levin, *American Marxism,* ISBN 978-1-15011-3597-2

101. CCS https://bit.ly/3szv6l3

102. Wikipedia https://bit.ly/3kgiPhp

103. Hutchinson Kansas, geological survey https://bit.ly/3hA9i59

104. Liberty County, Texas https://bit.ly/33UKYTL

Index

About the Author

Donn Dears

Donn Dears is a retired GE Company senior executive specializing in power generation, with extensive experience in Europe, the Mideast and Southeast Asia. He worked with government officials to obtain needed charters and authorizations to establish GE subsidiaries in fourteen countries to service large power generation and related electric apparatus.

The investment in Bahrain was the first investment GE had ever made in the Mideast, other than in sales offices. While modest, it led to larger investments later.

Donn began his career at General Electric as a test engineer testing large steam turbines and generators used by utilities to generate electricity. He then spent three years on GE's prestigious Manufacturing Management Program in diverse businesses, including locomotives, DC motors, medium steam turbines, small jet engines, and naval ordnance. This was followed by five years in manufacturing and marketing assignments at the Transformer Division.

He then led organizations servicing GE power generation and large equipment in the United States and then around the world.

Donn was involved with work done at customer locations, such as steel mills, electric utilities, refineries, oil drilling and production facilities and open pit and underground mining operations.

He subsequently led an engineering department providing engineering and technical support for GE organizations and subsidiaries around the world.

After retiring, Donn established a not-for-profit, then wrote several books and published articles on energy issues on the website Power For USA.

He has also been active in the community, serving two terms on the Reston Association Board of Directors, a large association with over 60,000 residents.

Donn has traveled extensively, beginning with a year at sea while a cadet-midshipman at the United States Merchant Marine Academy where he visited countries in Asia, Europe, and South America while still 19. He continues to travel and has visited over 60 countries on business and for pleasure.

Donn is a graduate of the United States Merchant Marine Academy, BS in engineering, with honors.

He served on active duty in the US Navy during the Korean War.

Made in United States
Orlando, FL
10 May 2022

17737986R00074